I0046707

When Numbers Don't Add Up

When Numbers Don't Add Up

Accounting Fraud and Financial Technology

Faisal Sheikh, BSc. (Hons), FCCA, FHEA, FFA, FIPA

BEP
BUSINESS EXPERT PRESS
Leader in applied, concise business books

When Numbers Don't Add Up: Accounting Fraud and Financial Technology
Copyright © Business Expert Press, LLC, 2021.

All rights reserved. No part of this publication may be reproduced, stored in a retrieval system, or transmitted in any form or by any means—electronic, mechanical, photocopy, recording, or any other except for brief quotations, not to exceed 250 words, without the prior permission of the publisher.

First published in 2021 by
Business Expert Press, LLC
222 East 46th Street, New York, NY 10017
www.businessexpertpress.com

ISBN-13: 978-1-94858-089-2 (paperback)
ISBN-13: 978-1-94858-090-8 (e-book)

Business Expert Press Financial Accounting, Auditing, and Taxation
Collection

Collection ISSN: 2151-2795 (print)
Collection ISSN: 2151-2817 (electronic)

Cover image licensed by Ingram Image, StockPhotoSecrets.com
Cover and interior design by S4Carlisle Publishing Services Private Ltd.,
Chennai, India

First edition: 2021

10 9 8 7 6 5 4 3 2 1

Printed in the United States of America.

Dedicated to

Fra Luca Pacioli,

Pir Muhammed Nur ud Din Uwaysi,

&

My friends for being there when I needed you most

Brian Leigh
Eileen Roddy
Martin Walsh
Kathy & Bernie Maguire
Ghulam Sorwar
Abdi Ali
Scott Isenberg
MUM, DAD
&
RUBY

Zahra, Maryam, Halimah, and my readers remember if you realize His face then:

"I swear, since seeing Your face,
the whole world is fraud and fantasy
The garden is bewildered as to what is leaf
or blossom. The distracted birds
can't distinguish the birdseed from the snare.

A house of love with no limits,
a presence more beautiful than Venus or the moon,
a beauty whose image fills the mirror of the heart."

~ Rumi

"Al Capone's bookkeeper once said that *he can steal more with a pencil than ten men with machine guns* — the situation is much worse today, with computers that have increased the speed, the possible scope of criminal acts and the difficulty to investigate such crimes."

Brinkley and Schell, cited in Abrams et al. 1995

Description

The book begins with a brief assessment of corporate crime, fraud in general, and how accounting fraud is different. There is a review of notorious cases such as Enron (2001) and recently Toshiba (2015), including the socioeconomic consequences of this nefarious crime. The author contextualized the phenomenon of accounting fraud using a framework he developed called "Corporate Governance Cosmos." Thereafter, the book contains an up-to-date literature review (in order to make the book more readable, academic references have been kept to an absolute minimum, but a full reference list is provided), beginning with a thorough appraisal and critique of the seminal theory in this area, namely, the Fraud Triangle and its different variations. There is a comprehensive exploration of the motivations for accounting fraud and a growing realization that Dark Triad (psychopathy, narcissism, and Machiavellianism) tendencies may explain why executives engage in accounting fraud. There is a small contribution to the literature by the author, who expands an established framework entitled Cooks Recipes Incentives Monitoring End results (C R I M E) by Rezaee (2005). The author extended it to C R I M E L, where L is the "Learning" from 33 international case studies of accounting fraud. Accountants, auditors, antifraud practitioners, and graduate students will find the mini case studies of accounting fraud particularly useful as it makes the phenomenon tangible and more understandable. The penultimate chapter is a study of the likely impact of financial technology on accounting fraud. The author concludes by pulling salient previous sections and philosophical ideas together, including a brief discussion of ethics, forwarding his International Code of Ethics for Professional Accountants (IFAC) Ethical Triangle, his vision for the future accountant, which he refers to as accounting engineers, and an ancient prescription for the curse of accounting fraud.

Keywords

accounting fraud; corporate governance cosmos; fraud triangle; dark triad; C R I M E L; financial technology; IFAC ethical triangle; accounting engineer

Contents

Acknowledgments

They say that literary projects take on a life of their own, and I brashly thought this book was going to take less than a year to write. Instead it has taken nearly two years, and I have experienced many highs and lows, even thinking, at one point, I would never complete this book. Hence, I remain indebted to friends and family for their care and support.

I remain deeply grateful to Business Expert Press, especially Scott and Shyam, for their support and patience. A big thank you to my colleagues who graciously agreed to write forewords and gave me very productive suggestions on how to improve the book—Richard Williams and Nigel Iyer. As ever, thanks to my close friend and mentor Brian Leigh, who meticulously proofread the text.

I have stolen time and energy from my wife and little girls, but, collectively, they are a testament to the fact that behind every successful man there is a woman, or in my case women.

I continue with my study of accounting fraud and would sincerely appreciate any experiences or feedback from my readers.

Thanks!

Faisal Sheikh
F.M.Sheikh@salford.ac.uk / Faisal.Masud.Sheikh@hotmail.com

Foreword: Audit Partner's Perspective

Fraudulent activities appear present in many aspects of life in the 21st century, whether manifested through "fake news," "scammers" using online trading platforms, or even professional sportspeople caught out "diving" or simulating foul play.

This is possibly facilitated by technological advances and may be more prevalent for us today than to previous generations. Or is this an illusion created by increased media exposure? What is certain is that fraud has been part of the human experience since time immemorial.

Faisal's book gives a detailed insight into one specific type of fraud, Accounting Fraud.

As an external auditor by profession, I will be quick to point to the author's reference that it is not the role of the external auditors to detect fraud. It is inevitable, however, that difficult questions will be asked of the auditors when financial wrongdoing comes to light. The resultant reputational damage makes this study a compelling read to anyone in the accountancy profession.

The author lifts the veil covering the murky world of accounting fraud. He looks at some of the headline grabbing accounting scandals of the last 20 years to explore the common themes and then moves on to examine the literature and theoretical works conducted to identify and define the circumstances that led to heightened vulnerabilities.

The book then provides case studies to demonstrate the sleight of hand required for seemingly innocent journals to turn losses to profits, pushing beyond the boundaries of a true and fair presentation of the company's performance. This provides a timely reminder of how a biased interpretation of Generally Accepted Accounting Principles (GAAP) by a suitably motivated CFO/CEO can quickly change the picture reported. We are then reminded that evidence supports CFO/CEO involvement in 80 percent of accounting fraud cases, emphasizing the point.

Finally, we are brought right up to date—into the fast-developing world of blockchain, Big Data, and the use of data-analytic tools within audit. Faisal puts forward a robust argument that we stand on the threshold of a new age of financial control. The days of sample-based substantive audit and even controls-based audit must surely be numbered, as computer-assisted audit tools (CAAT) can now handle data sets recording 100 percent of transactions. Interesting times ahead.

Richard Williams
Partner

Beever and Struthers
United Kingdom
http://www.beeverstruthers.co.uk/aboutus/richard_williams

Foreword: Counter-Fraud Practitioner's Assessment

Reducing and removing the impact of fraud and corruption is one of the big challenges we face in the world today, alongside, of course, eradicating poverty, promoting world peace, and cleaning up the environment. But unlike many of the other big global challenges, fraud and corruption is one part of human nature we *should* be easily able to avoid. It should be quite simple to deal with because cheating, stealing, and deception are nothing new...they have been around for centuries. But all the same, despite a tsunami of new rules and regulations in recent years, fraud is constantly on the increase. And what's more, corruption and fraud are the "dirt in our machinery," which get in the way of us overcoming many of the other global challenges that we as a human race are dealing with.

As Faisal writes in this highly educational and accessible book, "Fraud has perhaps existed since the beginning of trade and commerce... a very long time ago." Accounting fraud is a subset of fraud. In simple terms, it is "any kind of financial reporting deception." And it's nothing new. For example, in Roman times, accounting fraud occurred when one of Emperor Julius Caesars's provincial governors grossly underreported to Rome the value of assets in his province.... because he had, of course, stolen them. To detect this, the meticulous and rightly curious Caesar regularly sent out his Quaestors to audit his provincial assets and look for fraud. Any accounting fraud that was discovered would result in the severest penalty for the governor involved.

All over the world fraud and corruption is as common as the common cold. Accounting fraud has really spread like wildfire. It's time we asked some critical questions: Are today's accountants and auditors less meticulous and skeptical compared with their Roman Empire counterparts? Has some other factor, such as the rapid development of seamless and integrated financial technology or just too much data to be able to see the details, masked the ability of accountants and auditors to spot when the numbers don't add up? Or have we disguised the language of accounting in such complex jargon that only a few elite (or so called "forensic") accountants are able to spot fraud? Whatever the case, our world is today crying out for accountants and auditors to step up to the plate and take more responsibility to defend the world from accounting fraud. There is nothing scary about accounting fraud at all, and the more people who know what it is, the easier it is to spot.

The beauty of Faisal's book is that it demystifies accounting fraud for the everyday accountant, auditor, student, or aspiring amateur "fraud detective." Using simple language, he deconstructs numerous cases where the figures and/or the books have been falsified and crystallizes what we all can learn to both detect and prevent accounting deception and nip accounting fraud in the bud.

This book is a gift for *all* accountants, students of accounting, fraud investigators describing what the essence of accounting fraud is, cutting through the usual academic discussions around compliance, risk analysis, auditing, and procedures.

On a personal note, I hope that the large external auditor firms will take note of this book. Their own international audit standards talk about their responsibilities in respect of accounting fraud, which boils down to being professionally skeptical and assessing whether fraud is a risk on every audit performed. And if they decide that fraud is a risk, then their own standards say that they are supposed to do something to discover it. Of course, the current "get out of jail almost free" card for every external auditor is that they can decide, together with the management, that for each individual audit the risk of fraud is low. But the question remains, since fraud is so common how can the risk on almost every audit be low? So before rereading their own auditing standards, we would all benefit from external auditors also studying this book!

Nigel Iyer
Founder & Chairman
B4 Investigate
http://b4investigate.com/contact/

CHAPTER 1

The Growing Phenomenon of Accounting Fraud

To gain a deeper insight into why accounting fraud occurs, a thorough understanding of the concept is essential. Consequently, it is necessary to briefly explore the concept of white-collar crime, including corporate crime, which will give an overview of the phenomenon illustrated with important yet notorious accounting scandals such as Parmalat and ensuing consequences. This will provide a basis for further exploration of the significance, nature, and cost of accounting fraud.

Thereafter, the author will critically elaborate the important theoretical models of accounting fraud, beginning with the Donald Cressey's Fraud Triangle, including sociological and psychological approaches that attempt to explain why accounting fraud takes place.

Outline of Corporate Crime

As stated earlier, corporate crimes are white-collar crimes executed by corporations or an individual in a position of authority such as a CEO. This includes all corporate activities that are prohibited and punishable by law. It is argued that what is being sought are organizational benefits instead of individual gains. Many corporate crimes are highly complex, involving multiple actors, and it is difficult to establish who is responsible for the harm. It is maintained that most ordinary people are unaware of the frequency and economic damage caused by corporate crimes. The socioeconomic fallout from criminal activities committed by companies can be devastating, resulting in tens of thousands of job losses, as in the case of WorldCom. It should not be a surprise when some commentators deem corporate crime to be one of the gravest crimes that occur in society.

It is believed that corporate crime wreaks more socioeconomic destruction than all street crime combined and is even claimed that corporate crime is a form of violent crime. Many social problems, tyranny of native and indigenous communities, food contamination, medical negligence, and unsafe working conditions, are a result of concerted corporate power. Furthermore, many of the penalties imposed on corporations have little or no impact on their finances and business practices; hence the requirement for alternative methods of restricting and effectively controlling corporate crime.

The author will now focus on the understanding, modeling, and analysis of accounting fraud. Hence, an overview of the accounting fraud phenomenon follows, including a review of the most notorious accounting scandals of modern times as evidence of the socioeconomic impact of fraudulent financial reporting or accounting fraud.

What Is Fraud?

Fraud has existed perhaps since the beginning of trade and commerce. According to some experts, basic body measurements and calculations or biometrics were used thousands of years ago as a method of gauging the trustworthiness of traders, implying that dishonest businesspeople have always existed. In general, fraud includes the intent to deceive, breaking the rule of law or established norms or protocols such as accounting standards, resulting in negative, if not harmful, consequences to its victims. KPMG (2017) noted that "[t]he total cost of fraudulent activity in the UK has surpassed a billion pounds (£1.1 billion) for the first time since 2011."

The Oxford Dictionary describes fraud in the following way:

> "Wrongful or criminal deception intended to result in financial or personal gain."

The above definition describes the fundamental nature of fraud but does not explain its nature and features. As already discussed, fraud is not a recent trend, nor is it limited to humankind. Animals also engage in what could be argued, at minimum, as manipulative behavior or fraudulent activities, such as chameleons changing color. A more comprehensive definition of fraud is supplied by Van Vlasselaer et al. (2016):

"Fraud is an uncommon, well-considered, imperceptibly concealed, time-evolving and often carefully organized crime which appears in many types of form."

Why Companies Produce Financial Statements and How Accounting Fraud Is Different

Financial statements are prepared because they assist in decision making, planning, and controlling processes. In most of the world it is also a statutory requirement to produce financial statements according to country-specific Generally Accepted Accounting Principles (GAAP) such as U.S. GAAP or International Financial Reporting Standards. Furthermore, the financial statements are vital tools for senior managers, because they help to communicate past achievements and are a basis for future expectations or plans. The figures reported in the financial statements provide an important source of information regarding the evaluation of performance, going concern, and the story of the company's history. Thus, the accuracy of these documents is exceedingly important because they reflect the actual financial position of a company at any given time. External stakeholders such as analysts scrutinize the financial information supplied by financial statements in order to consider the financial performance of the company and make investments/recommendations accordingly. Specifically, equity investors and creditors will be concerned with the quality and sustainability of profitability and cash flow, these being the key sources of financing for the operation of the company. Financial statements for public listed companies are authenticated by both internal and external auditors in order to give more reliability to the reported financial position.

Jackson (2015) suggests that accounting fraud (also referred to as "corporate fraud" or "financial reporting fraud" or "financial statement fraud") is a special kind of fraud that necessitates the manipulation of financial statements. The Association of Certified Fraud Examiners (ACFE) is a renowned American professional antifraud body that globally provides antifraud training and education. In the ACFEs 2018 Fraud Examiners Manual, accounting fraud is defined as "the deliberate misrepresentation of the financial condition of an enterprise accomplished through the intentional misstatement or omission of amounts or disclosures in the financial statements to deceive financial statement users." It is suggested that the first recorded example of accounting fraud was the one that occurred in the 1600s to the British East India Company. Others argue that accounting fraud does not result in an explicit financial advantage to anyone. Instead, it supplies an implicit gain, in the shape of higher share prices, superior stock options for managers, and continued lines of credit.

Major corporate scandals have occurred that have shaken the confidence of all stakeholders, the public, and investors, and, worryingly in the financial system itself. The phenomenon of accounting fraud underpinned almost all cases of recent corporate scandals such as, the UK-based, Carillion in 2018. It is argued that when financial statements are not accurate as a result of accounting irregularities, they change from a highly useful tool into a way of deceiving the public.

Research suggests that unethical conduct and fraudulent activities such as manipulation of accounting information does not occur in a vacuum; rather, there must be specific factors that make it possible. It is claimed that most examples of corporate failure occur for various reasons, including fraudulent financial reporting, misuse of power, insider trading, corruption, bribery, unsuitable investment practices, pursuing short-term profits to the detriment of shareholders, poor internal control environment, and ineffective management.

Leading fraud examiner Wells (2005a,b) argues that fraud is not merely an accounting problem but a social phenomenon and that there are three methods of unlawfully taking money from a victim, namely, by force, stealth, or trickery. Hence, a weak internal control environment in an organization is an opportunity for a fraudster. Where an accounting information system does not supply timely, accurate, sufficiently detailed, and relevant results, it is susceptible to theft and concealment from the company bank account. A weak internal audit function, or lack of one, is also a sign of poor internal control. A specific example of deficient accounting practice is failure to ensure monthly bank reconciliations.

Accounting Scandals

The spectacular rise of corporate accounting scandals at the start of the 21st century has exacerbated the phenomenon of accounting fraud that causes corporate bankruptcy, unnecessary market corrections, and socioeconomic malaise. The following examples are the most notorious instances of accounting fraud scandals that highlight the unintended consequences of unethical behavior.

Enron, 2001

Enron Corporation, founded in 1985, was a large energy company that was engaged in an enormous fraudulent scheme that climaxed in 2001 when the company suffered the largest Chapter 11 bankruptcy in history (since exceeded by WorldCom during 2002 and Lehman Brothers during 2008).

Enron was a darling of the stock market and had been considered a blue-chip stock investment, so this was an unparalleled event in the financial world. Enron's passing occurred after the revelation that the bulk of its profits and revenue were the result of deals with special purpose entities. Thus, many of Enron's debts and the losses that it suffered were not reported in its financial statements, i.e., accounting fraud. At the end of 2001, it was discovered that Enron's financial statements were underpinned by institutionalized, systematic, and creatively planned accounting fraud.

The main actors in the debacle were Chairman Jen Kay, CEO Jeffrey Skilling, and CFO Andrew Fastow, who engaged in highly aggressive off-balance sheet finance that resulted in billions of dollars in long-term debt being kept off the records. Ultimately, the figures did not correlate, and the inevitable decrease in net income led to an estimated billion-dollar reduction in the equity of shareholders. As expected, investors reacted negatively, and quickly Enron's stock price collapsed, from US$90.56 during the summer of 2000 to just pennies (January 11, 2002—$0.12), quickening the company's bankruptcy. Enron's shareholders lost nearly $74 billion, and 4,500 employees lost their jobs and pension funds without proper notice.

It is argued that the fiasco could have been avoided if previous financial statements had been forensically examined. The remarkable revenue growth from $9.2 billion in 1995 to $100.8 billion in 2000 should have warned interested stakeholders that this was not underpinned by a similar increase in profitability.

The scandal highlighted aggressive accounting practices and activities of many corporations in the United States and was a major factor in the enactment of the Sarbanes–Oxley Act of 2002. The scandal also affected the wider business world by causing the closure of the renowned audit firm Arthur Andersen, which had been in business for nearly 100 years and was Enron's main auditor.

WorldCom, 2002

Less than a year after the financial earthquake caused by Enron, another scandal shook the markets in the telecommunication services supplier WorldCom, now known as MCI.

According to the U.S. Securities and Exchange Commission (SEC) (2003), company CEO Bernard Ebbers, CFO Scott Sullivan, Controller David Myers, and Director of General Accounting Buford Yates used duplicitous accounting techniques to conceal its decreasing earnings to maintain the price of WorldCom's share price.

The fraud was executed by capitalizing rather than expensing approximately $3.8 billion of expenditure and inflating revenues with false accounting entries, creating an image of growth in order to exaggerate profits. The company filed for bankruptcy protection shortly after the revelation of the fraudulent scheme, causing 17,000 redundancies and losses of $180 billion.

Adelphia, 2002

Adelphia was local cable franchise that was transformed by John Rigas into a giant of the telecommunications industry that included high-speed Internet, cable, and long-distance telephone service. During May 2002, Adelphia declared earnings restatement for 2000 and 2001, which included billions of dollars in off-balance sheet liabilities linked with "coborrowing agreements." The financial statements of Adelphia highlighted a myriad of issues. According to the last 10-K filed by the company (for the year ended December 31, 2000) it showed a net loss of $548 million; of $21.5 billion in total assets, of which $14.1 billion were intangibles, liabilities totaled $16.3 billion and equity was a modest

$4.2 billion. Adelphia subsequently filed for bankruptcy in June 2002, after being investigated by the SEC, which resulted in company executives being charged with accounting fraud: "Adelphia, at the direction of the individual defendants: (1) fraudulently excluded billions of dollars of liabilities from its consolidated financial statements by hiding them in off-balance-sheet affiliates; (2) falsified operation statistics and inflated Adelphia's earnings to meet Wall Street expectations; and (3) concealed rampant self-dealing by the Rigas family" (Gao, 2002:122).

At the heart of the accounting fraud were false transactions, with supporting documents suggesting that debts were repaid; instead, they were transferred to affiliates. In addition, the company was run as a personal fiefdom by the Rigas family, who, for example, used company funds to buy stock for the Rigas family and even built a golf club. It is important to note that five members of the nine-member board were John Rigas's immediate relatives, including his son, who was CFO, suggesting poor corporate governance and management override was potentially endemic in the company. Eventually, two former Adelphia executives were charged with criminal charges for conspiracy, bank fraud, and securities fraud. In 2004 John Rigas and his son were both convicted of conspiracy and fraud.

Global Crossing, 2002

Global Crossing was an integrated telecommunications solutions company that was founded in 1997 by an investment banker called Gary Winnick. Its headquarters were in Bermuda, but it operated primarily in the United States and 27 other countries and in excess of 200 cities across the globe. After a series of accounting indiscretions, the company announced Chapter 11 Bankruptcy Protection on January 28, 2002. Investors, analysts, and regulators were left stunned as Global Crossing was considered a darling of the market. The Chapter 11 statement also announced that two companies, namely, Hutchinson Whampoa and Singapore Technologies Telemedia (STT), had signed a letter of intent that they would inject a $750-million cash investment in exchange for a combined majority share of 60 percent or more in the business.

A closer inspection of the financial statements revealed mounting debts of $12 billion coupled with unsecured creditors and affiliates numbering over one thousand. The latter covered a wide spectrum of lenders, equipment vendors, and other carriers. U.S. Trust Co., one of the secured creditors, was owed $3.6 billion, approximately 25 percent of Global Crossing's total debts. The company was highly valued on the market but had a poor cash flow and working capital position. The company had engaged in a dubious and complex earnings management technique, called "capacity swaps." Global Crossing would record traffic on other fiber-optic telecommunications systems such as Qwest and in return booked traffic on its own network. Thus, each counterparty in this complex accounting fraud reported an increase in recorded revenue, although there was no actual increase in economic activity. The swaps were also undertaken to conceal different costs and exceed market expectations. Global Crossing went on to lure more customers and investors by overstating the reach and attractiveness of its network. However, this was not underpinned by sound financials, including profitability and crucially cash flow, which is the lifeblood of any business. Consequently, Global Crossing became highly leveraged with unsustainable levels of liabilities coupled with questionable assets and became the largest telecom bankruptcy filing ever,—the fourth largest of any kind in American corporate history. Unfortunately, the company was also plagued by poor governance, and even after its bankruptcy it lent $15 million to John Legere, its then CEO, and, surprisingly, agreed to let him keep the money if he stayed on until February 2003.

Parmalat S.p.A, 2004

Parmalat S.p.A was an Italian multinational dairy and food company and at one time became the leading global producer of long-life milk, but the company folded in 2003 with a £13-billion hole in its financial statements in what remains Europe's biggest liquidation to date. The SEC (2003) described the European scandal as "one of the largest and most brazen corporate financial frauds in history." The Parmalat was an example of accounting fraud that was achieved by several factors, including a weak corporate governance structure and lack of professional care by external auditors and was exacerbated by the greed of senior management. Calisto Tanzi, founder and CEO of Parmalat, was prone to greed and unethical behavior, for example, redirecting Parmalat's monies to a company managed by his daughter, Francesca Tanzi (Ogutu, 2016). An investigation reported that Tanzi diverted approximately €500 million to Permatour, a company that his daughter managed. Furthermore, it is suggested that what happened at Parmalat was premeditated and a flagrant misstatement of information with the intent to misinform.

It was reported that Parmalat defaulted on a $185-million bond payment in November 2002, causing its auditors and bankers to examine the company's consolidated accounts. This examination found that approximately 38 percent of company assets were allegedly held in a $4.9-billion Bank of America account of a company subsidiary in the Cayman Islands. However, in December 2002, the Bank of America reported that no account for this Parmalat subsidiary ever existed. Italian prosecutors stated that they had discovered that Parmalat management merely concocted assets to offset nearly $16.2 billion of liabilities and blatantly fabricated financial statements over a 15-year period, eventually driving Parmalat into insolvency.

Lehman Brothers, 2008

In 2008 Lehman Brothers filed for the largest Chapter 11 bankruptcy in history, with $639 billion in assets and $619 billion in debt. At the time Lehman Brothers was the fourth-largest U.S. investment bank, and after its demise 25,000 employees globally lost their jobs.

It is contended that legitimate accounting standards were misinterpreted coupled with accounting fraud to prepare and disclose financial statements according to the desire of Lehman Brother's senior management. Lehman Brothers did not show important transactions in the notes to the financial statements, causing some commentators to argue for the review of Generally Accepted Accounting Standards. At the crux of the accounting fraud was the aggressive employment of an accounting technique referred to as Repo 15 (Morin and Maux, 2011:42):

"On March 12, 2010, a 2,200 page enquiry report prepared by legal expert Anton R. Valukas revealed the extensive use of accounting manipulations that might have largely contributed to the collapse of Lehman Brothers, which went bankrupt on September 15, 2008. This report sheds light on the systematic use of a balance sheet window-dressing technique called Repo 105, which let Lehman remove approximately $50 billion in commitments from its balance sheet in June 2008, and artificially reduce its net debt level by wagering on the collateralized loan market."

Experts believed that Ernst & Young deliberately ignored balance sheet shenanigans as early as the early 2000s. If the cash flow statement had been analyzed, the accounting fraud could have been identified and potentially corrected.

Toshiba, 2015

In 2015, the CEO of Toshiba Corporation (Toshiba) resigned over the revelation of a JP¥151.8-billion accounting fraud that shocked the financial world. The accounting fraud was reported to be US$1.2 billion of earnings manipulation through window dressing; it later escalated to US$2 billion from 2008 to 2014.

Just like the Lehman 2008 scandal, legitimate accounting standards were abused to inflate revenue. Toshiba's operating profit was overstated by approximately US$4.1 billion from March 2012 to February 2015. This was due to the abuse of an accounting method called "percentage-of-completion," which is routinely utilized in long-term projects. According to this method, sales and expenses are established in an accounting period completed to date. To deal with the intense media and public scrutiny, Toshiba set up a panel to investigate the extent of the accounting fraud. Toshiba asserted that the problem was caused by big civil engineering projects such as electricity generation and railways, where managers had decided on achieving profit targets by dishonestly reducing expenses. The managers' biased judgements, coupled with the knowledge of auditors, resulted in overstated sales and profits and corresponding understatements of expenses, including adjustments to goodwill. Toshiba continues to face class lawsuits from shareholders, and the proud brand with a 140-year history lies in tatters.

Thus far it is apparent that accounting fraud occurs because of multiple factors, including greed and misinterpreting or aggressively applying accounting standards, all in a bid to maintain profitability and, ultimately, a stable and growing share price. These latter factors will be fully explored in Chapter 2.

Accounting fraud causes major damage to internal and external stakeholders such as investors, employees, and society at large. Accounting fraud occurs in approximately 10 percent of internal fraud cases; however, the median cost of accounting fraud is $975k in comparison with asset misappropriation that has a median loss of $125k in 83.5 percent of cases (ACFE, 2016). Analysts suggest that major accounting scandals, for example Enron, have increased the concerns of investors in accounting fraud. The Chairman of the SEC commented in the aftermath of the global financial crunch that:

> "One of the fundamental requirements for rational investing and efficient capital formation is the availability of high-quality information. One of our core functions is collecting and making publicly available financial and other relevant information from public companies."

Hence, the well-being of financial markets is dependent on the production of robust financial information, i.e., financial statements.

Overview of Accounting Fraud

Following notorious fraud scandals as outlined in previous sections, investors' concerns about fraud, in general, and accounting or financial statement fraud has risen. Hence, this section aims to provide an outline of accounting fraud, including its nature, economic impact, types, and how it is perpetrated.

Sheikh (2017) created a useful framework to examine corporate governance salient to the study of accounting fraud, called the Corporate Governance Cosmos; see Figure 1.1. He reminds us that the primary objective of a company is to maximize profits and therefore enhance the wealth of its shareholders. This is achieved by utilizing internally generated accounting information, which informs decision making. The important questions that arise during the potentially incongruent pursuit of profit and wealth maximization are who exercises responsibility and accountability, and what relationships and possible conflicts exist between "principals" and their "agents," i.e., the agency problem.

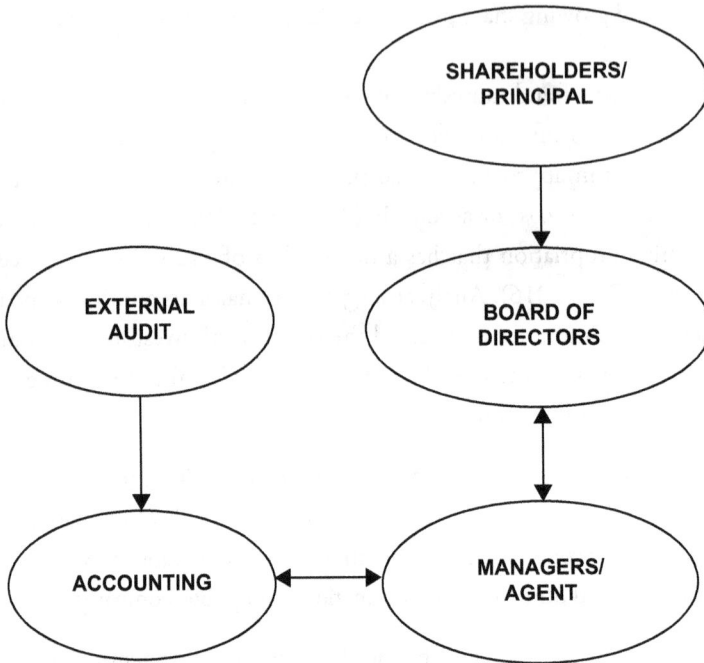

Figure 1.1 Corporate Governance Cosmos

Shareholders are known as the "principal," and the directors are the "agents." Experts in corporate governance suggest that the extent to which boards of directors act in the interests of shareholders and in the execution of their fiduciary duties such as wealth maximization is established by which of the seven perspectives is taken on corporate social responsibility.

The groundbreaking study of Jensen and Meckling (1976) established that the principal–agent problem arises when a principal produces an environment in which an agent's incentives are incongruous with those of the principal. The burden is on the principal to create incentives or mechanisms for the agent to make certain that they behave as the principal desires, for example, to maximize shareholder wealth. This includes financial incentives to avoid information asymmetry such as overvalued equity. It is argued that *managerial opportunism* is a major determinant in these scandals, for example, managers who are remunerated for short-term results will potentially report misleading information, i.e., accounting fraud, because short-term gains outweigh the long-term ones such as pension obligations. An extreme example of asymmetric information and agency cost is when an executive is aware of a takeover and secretly facilitates the sale of the company at a lower price by engineering a lower share price by releasing poor results to the market or convincing shareholders regarding the sale. Later, the executive is handsomely rewarded by a golden handshake for managing the sale.

As noted earlier, accounting information is generated internally, and therefore the role of external audit is to dampen moral hazard and the abuse of asymmetric information by the agents, i.e., accounting fraud. It is not the role of external auditors to detect fraud, but it is considered the norm that they have an active function in it. External audit promotes assurance and emphasizes trust in the financial information produced by companies. On the other hand, external auditors may be held liable if an accounting fraud case is not discovered, and this phenomenon is known as the "audit expectations gap." In view of a growing number of accounting fraud scandals, there is significant demand on the audit profession, by professional accountancy bodies, to improve audit quality and, by extension, accounting fraud detection. Despite this, research suggests that the external auditors are still deficient at assessing accounting fraud.

In recent years the study of accounting fraud has grown significantly, and therefore the detection of financial fraud has become an ever more demanding and important task. It is argued that accounting fraud detection requires the collective work of "corporate governance professionals," namely, the board of directors, the audit committee, senior management, and internal and external auditors. It is suggested that understanding the various strands of accounting fraud should enable external auditors to better gauge the fraud risks inherent in an economic entity. However, this does not explain why accounting fraud continues.

Woodcock (2015) suggests that in spite of the Sarbanes–Oxley Act of 2002, major improvements in internal controls, "Many Eyes Are On the Lookout for Fraud" including academics; analysts; and regulators incentivizing the reporting/whistleblowing of accounting fraud through the Dodd-Frank Act 2014, accounting fraud persists. This is the motivation for the current study to explore why accounting fraud continues unabated.

The Significance and Cost of Accounting Fraud

Accounting fraud occurs when financial reports materially misrepresent the information or when material facts are not fully disclosed in such reports. Accounting fraud has also been referred to as "management fraud" because it is probably undertaken by management, for example in Enron, where executives were charged with creating complex accounting schemes to make Enron look more profitable to facilitate personal gains. This has been acknowledged by International Standard on Auditing (ISA) No. 240, The Auditor's Responsibilities Relating to Fraud in an Audit of Financial Statements:

> "Management is in a unique position to perpetrate fraud because of management's ability to manipulate accounting records and prepare fraudulent financial statements by overriding controls that otherwise appear to be operating effectively. Due to the unpredictable way in which such override could occur, it is regarded as a significant risk of material misstatement due to fraud" (2009:31).

Accounting fraud involves deliberate omissions or nondisclosures in financial statements that are intended to mislead users of financial statements. Researchers argue that accounting fraud is the intentional attempt by companies to mislead users of financial statements by producing materially misstated company accounts.

Analysts found that the share price of a company fell steeply once it became public knowledge that it had engaged in accounting fraud, such as with the UK listed company Tesco in 2017, which admitted that its 2014 profits were overstated by £250 million. The consequences of accounting fraud are far-reaching and can lead to erosion of investors' confidence in the audit profession and the capital markets, damaging companies and forcing them to hire new managers, with overall harm to the economy and society.

The ACFE (2016) study highlighted that accounting fraud usually occurs in larger companies, particularly in construction, banking and financial services, health care, and manufacturing. The report also, worryingly, stated that the number of accounting fraud case has risen since the previous report in 2014.

The next chapter will briefly discuss the types of accounting fraud techniques mentioned in the literature and introduce the original model that purports to explain fraud in general, which can also be applied to accounting fraud. This model will be critiqued and extended to incorporate the "Dark Triad" (narcissism, Machiavellianism, and psychopathy).

CHAPTER 2

The Fraud Literature

The Fraud Triangle has been extensively applied by both researchers and regulators in order to prevent and detect fraud. Over the years, accounting researchers have updated the Fraud Triangle, resulting in extended models that purport to better understand the nature of fraud.

The three constituents of the Fraud Triangle (Pressure, Opportunity, Rationalization) have been successfully integrated by important regulators and professional bodies in the United States, where it is the bedrock of the

- Association of Certified Fraud Examiners' (ACFE) *"Fraud Examiners Manual"*;
- the Public Company Accounting Oversight Boards' (PCAOB) AU Section 316, *"Consideration of Fraud in a Financial Statement Audit"*;
- and the American Institute of Certified Public Accountants' (AICPA) SAS no. 99, *"Consideration of Fraud in a Financial Statement Audit."*

This chapter will not only consider the appropriate literature, but will also attempt to synthesize the literature about accounting fraud, beginning with differential association theory, then the Fraud Triangle, and the Dark Triad located in organizational deviance. This will enable a better understanding of accounting fraud and the fraud models. However, it is important to understand the major types of accounting fraud.

The Types of Accounting Fraud, Including Techniques

Accounting fraud centers on inappropriate revenue recognition, hidden liabilities and expenses, inappropriate asset valuation, and inappropriate disclosure. ACFE (2018) divided fraud schemes into three distinct categories: Misappropriation of Assets, Bribery/Corruption Fraud, and Fraudulent Financial Statements, which are together known as the "Fraud Tree." According to the ACFE (2018:10) Report to the Nations, Table 2.1:

Table 2.1 ACFE (2018) report to the nations

	% of Cases	Median Loss
Asset Misappropriation	89	$114,000
Corruption	38	$250,000
Financial Statement Fraud	10	$800,000

(Adapted from ACFE (2018) by author)

The misappropriation of assets accounts for the largest percentage of fraud cases, at 89 percent. On the other hand, the median losses of the asset misappropriation are the lowest in comparison with the other schemes. Although financial statement fraud or accounting fraud accounts for the lowest number of cases, it results in the highest financial harm.

Researchers discovered that inappropriate revenue and inappropriate asset valuation were the most frequent techniques for performing accounting fraud. Others found that the type of accounting fraud was dependent on the industry, and thus, for example, revenue overstatements were more common in the technology industry, whereas asset overstatements occurred more frequently in financial services.

Inappropriate Revenue Recognition

Recording invented revenue and/or fraudulently inflating revenues is the simplest form of accounting fraud. The most notorious example of inappropriate revenue recognition was Enron, which had overstated earnings by more than $500 million and had created a web of Special-Purpose Entities (SPEs) to keep debt off its balance sheet. It is acknowledged there are three major types of fraudulent revenue management, namely, fictitious revenues, premature revenue recognition, and manipulation of adjustments to revenues. Box below summarizes these abusive techniques:

Examples of techniques used to abuse revenue

Techniques
Recognizing returned goods after the end of the reporting period
Writing off bad debts in later periods
Dishonest cutoff of sales transactions at the end of the reporting period
Not writing off bad debts
Exaggerating revenue
Nonrecording of returned goods from customers
Debiting bank transfers as cash received from customers
Recognizing gross revenue instead of net revenue
Not recording discounts agreed with customers
Treating consignment sales as completed sales
Recording sales that have not been sent or only partly sent
Early recognition of sales
Recording sales but holding up shipment to customers (known as bill and hold)
Altering the nature of a sales agreement that violates GAAP, such as unlimited return of goods if not sold by the customer
Concealing sales returns and allowances, resulting in the overstatement of revenue
Minimizing bad debt expense by manipulating the allowance for doubtful debts
Erroneous sales supported by false documentation
Misleading the percentage of completion, such as in long construction contracts
Unofficial shipments
Creating fraudulent sales and sending them to customers after the end of the reporting period
Manipulation of the cutoff date of sales so that the following period's sales are recognized in the current income statement

Inappropriate Asset Recognition

Manipulation of assets is undertaken to enhance the Statement of Financial Position or Balance Sheet, including significant ratios relating to assets such as the Return on Capital Employed. Box below summarizes the nefarious methods:

Examples of techniques to undertake asset valuation misuse

Techniques
Using market value rather than book value when recording the amounts related to mergers or acquisitions
Inappropriate valuation of investments by deliberately misclassifying the investments
Overstatement of the value of closing inventory by not writing off out-of-date or nonsalable inventory
Altering the method for valuing closing inventory
Manipulating overheads that are part of the calculation of closing inventory
Misstating depreciation by changing the useful economic life of the asset
Inappropriate recognition of inventory on consignment
Exaggerating the quantity of closing inventory by creating false journal entries
Overstating discounts
Inappropriately capitalizing inventory and start-up costs
Not properly accounting for inventory by not deducting costs of goods sold
Failure to write off obsolete inventory or other assets with impaired values
Overstating unit costs that are used to calculate inventory
Misleading the physical closing inventory count
Overstating the value of property, plant, and equipment
Exaggerating returns or recording returns in earlier periods
Not recording the correct value of marketable securities or assets with the help of related parties
Nonrecording of depreciation
Fraudulently managing reserves
Misstating estimates of fair market values
Recording non-verifiable assets that enhance a company's balance sheet
Exaggerating or recording fake accounts receivable
Not writing off accounts receivable as bad debts

Hidden Liabilities and Expenses

In comparison with improper revenue recognition, hiding liabilities or expenses is much easier to commit. Omitted transactions are usually more difficult to detect than inappropriately recorded ones, because there is no audit trail. The best method of concealing a debit such as pilfering cash is to miss a credit to keep things balanced, for example by minimizing liabilities.

Another technique for hiding liabilities and expenses is to capitalize them, resulting in higher earnings and assets. The fixed assets will be depreciated over the useful economic life of the asset, meaning that the cost is distributed over time. The most infamous example of the latter was carried out by WorldCom, which capitalized huge amounts of costs. Box below summarizes these malevolent practices:

Examples of hiding liabilities and expenses

Techniques
Nonrecognition of liabilities such as deferred revenues or contingent liabilities.
Minimizing accounts payable by deferring to further periods or falsifying reductions or preventing genuine changes
Booking cost of sales as another expense so it does not adversely affect gross margin
Capitalizing immaterial expenses that will probably not be detected
Reporting lower expenses by nondisclosure of sales discounts, returns, and allowances
Failure to correctly write down assets such as accounts receivable or closing inventory as per generally accepted accounting principles (GAAP)
Failure to record expenses as they occur
Failure to accrue genuine liabilities or record them in later periods
Booking deferred revenues as earned revenues
Failure to record repurchase agreements or commitments
Minimizing and recording low contingent liabilities
Misclassifying long-term liabilities as current liabilities and vice versa, resulting in superior ratios
Failure to record purchases
Exaggerating purchase returns and discounts

Inappropriate Disclosure

Most accounting fraud is related to the deliberate misstatement or omission of figures rather than disclosures. On the other hand, it is suggested that improper disclosure normally occurs in the following manner: liability omissions, subsequent events, related party transaction and accounting changes. For example, in regard to the Enron debacle it was contended that the company did not sufficiently reveal commitments to SPEs. Several studies have established that related party transactions usually take place in companies with poor governance and poor monitoring protocols, which only exacerbate risky behavior such as overstating reported income. However, in the case of loans to related parties (such as directors and officers), which are disallowed by Sarbanes Oxley, regulators do not prohibit related party transactions but expect disclosure. Coenen (2009) lists the following examples of falsifications or nondisclosures:

- Changes in estimates or between prior period accounting rules, resulting in the noncomparability of prior periods
- Presence of related party transactions or agreements that may not have been negotiated at arm's length
- Significant incidents occurring after the close of an accounting period that may result in a substantial impact on the judgments of financial statement users
- Undecided litigation or government scrutiny
- Probable product liability or major warranty concerns
- Major environmental changes causing a downturn in demand for products or services
- Reliance on outdated technology when the company has historically used cutting-edge technology that underpinned growing revenues
- Significant decrease in the market value of investments held by the company.

Corporate Governance and Accounting Fraud

According to the Financial Reporting Council (2016), corporate governance is the method by which organizations are directed and controlled. Boards of directors are accountable for the governance of their companies by creating official and clear protocols for ensuring equitable financial reporting, coupled with strong risk management and internal control systems/culture. Shareholders engage with the directors and the auditors to ensure that a suitable governance model is established. The role of detecting and, above all, preventing fraud is in the remit of management and those charged with governance.

A weak internal control system coupled with poor governance could increase the likelihood of accounting fraud, which is supported by the global 2018 ACFE fraud study. This also highlighted another signifi-cant factor, "ineffective board leadership," which could increase the risk of fraud. Several studies established a positive correlation between poor corporate governance and accounting fraud. It was discovered that the risk of accounting fraud dampens when there are more external directors on the board with vested interests in the company. Accounting fraud is more likely to happen when power remains solely in the hands of insid-ers because they have access to asymmetric information, which informs decision making.

According to International Standard on Auditing 240 (The Auditors Responsibility Relating to Fraud in an Audit of Financial Statements) (2010), external auditors have several objectives in relation to fraud:

A) To identify and assess the risks of material misstatement of the finan-cial statements due to fraud;
B) To obtain enough appropriate audit evidence regarding the assessed risks of material misstatement due to fraud, through designing and implementing appropriate responses; and
C) To respond appropriately to fraud or suspected fraud identified dur-ing the audit.

ISA 240 also requires external auditors to assess and respond to the risk of accounting fraud and to categorize that risk into three categories: risk of motives/pressure to commit fraud, risk of opportunity to com-mit fraud, and risk of rationalization of fraud (187:A125), i.e., the Fraud Triangle, which will be extensively discussed when exploring the motiva-tions for fraud.

External auditors may be held liable if companies unexpectedly go out of business or if it is found that important personnel are involved in fraud. However, it is important to acknowledge that there is an *audit expectations gap,* which is defined as the gap between what the society expects from external auditors and what it gains, although ISAs supply little guidance to external auditors with respect to the risk assessment of fraud. They can act as a valuable buffer against fraud, because most fraudsters are afraid of being exposed and of the related penalties. A recent study established the link between audit committee features and the consistency of financial reporting. The study also found that the risk of accounting fraud reporting is negatively correlated with audit committee independence and frequency of audit committee meetings, i.e., the latter mechanism deters accounting fraud.

It is argued that the audit expectation gap can be reduced by enhancing fraud risk assessment and employing better fraud detection methods. ISA 240 insists that external auditors utilize professional skepticism or doubt while ascertaining the risk of fraud. However, it is contended that professional doubt is not enough and that the external auditors need to use "critical thinking," which necessitates an appreciation of the motivations behind accounting fraud. This leads into the next section, where the author will examine the key motivations, theories, and approaches behind the phenomenon of accounting fraud.

Differential Association Theory

According to researchers, the causes and deterrence studies of crime have been the subject of extensive research in the fields of biology, sociology, criminology, psychology, and law. Theoretical models of crime can be categorized in three ways: biological, sociological, and classical and rational choice (Gottfredson and Hirschi, 1990). Classical and rational choice theorists argue that people have free will and are "rational calculators," who conduct cost-benefit analyses whenever they act, including criminal activities, whereas biological theorists contend that some people are "born into crime" owing to genetics and a predisposition to violent or criminal behavior. Finally, sociological theories of crime suggest that crime is caused by external factors, people's relationships with other people and/or organizations such as the school in their life. The most important sociological theories range from social learning theory to differential association theory. Differential association theory underpins the development of Cressey's Fraud Triangle theory. Rationalization, the third part of the Fraud Triangle, was derived from Sutherlands (1937) differential association theory, which argued that rationalization helps a criminal to justify their act. However, this rationalization was modified by Cressey (1953), who stated that fraudsters needed to satisfy themselves that they were behaving uprightly before they undertook the fraudulent act, which was theft, in Cressey's study. Differential association theory is also important in this study because it was created to describe crime in general, including financial and organized, and is not restricted to merely explaining the phenomenon of delinquent crime.

The theory of differential association, as articulated by Sutherland in 1939, contends that aberrant behavior is "learned behavior" and, crucially, how people become criminals. It is a general causal theory of crime that identifies specific conditions or circumstances that must occur for any crime to take place and therefore not present when crime does not happen. Hence, the theory of differential association is comprised of the following interconnected notions: (a) normative conflict, (b) differential association, and (c) differential association organization (Cressey, 1960), which function at the (i) societal or macro and (ii) individual or micro levels.

According to the differential association theory, crime is initiated by normative conflicts, where various factions in society are in conflict regarding norms, values, and interests. According to Matsueda (1988), at the "macro level," some groups accept that a certain rule should be adhered to no matter what the situation; in contrast, other groups state the exact rule should be breached in all circumstances, whereas other groups suggest that the same rule should be broken only in certain circumstances; this normative and legal conflict results in high crime rates. At the "micro level," criminal conduct is learned in the process of differential association via interaction with other people, including contemporaries in close groups.

The curriculum of learning comprises of (a) the methods and competences of undertaking crimes and (b) the necessary reason, rationalization, and mindset. The second set of learning is very influential because it dictates the bases of whether a specific rule should be obeyed or defied. As the normative conflict is taking place at the macro level, people, deliberately or unintentionally, are related with and, importantly, learn from those explaining or defining whether the rule should be adhered to or not. Thus, Sutherland concluded that criminal behavior takes place when people learn a surplus of explanations that support violating the rule (Sutherland and Cressey, 1960). However, it is important to note that these explanations are affected by occurrence, length, importance, and concentration. Thus, during differential association development, definitions will carry degrees of weight, so, for example, those explanations that are met more often, for a longer period, earlier in life, and from a significant person or a close associate will receive more credence and have more of an effect on someone's behavior. This body of literature has had a major impact on studies exploring adolescent delinquency located in "peer learning" (Piquero et al., 2005) and financial crimes based on differential association theory.

The Fraud Triangle

It is an interesting fact that Donald Cressey was a student of Sutherland and began his research in 1950 when he was exploring "criminal violation of financial trust." Cressey interviewed 250 prisoners over 5 months in the state of Illinois who fulfilled two criteria: (a) the person had accepted a position of trust and (b) the same person went on to violate this trust and undertake a crime. He was attempting to develop a general theory of criminal behavior, and his hypothesis was **underpinned by differential association theory**: the violation of financial trust occurred because of learned behavior during the normal course of business or professional activities, or the misdemeanors resulted during business or professional activities and had not been learned. This hypothesis was rejected because social learning did not appear to explain the crimes. Furthermore, many of the prisoners stated that they knew what they were doing was unlawful and incorrect. Moreover, they explained that they had operated in isolation and did not know anybody else who had committed such crimes in their business or profession. Cressey adapted the original hypothesis and concluded that three factors were necessary for the criminal violation of trust to take place: (a) a "non-shareable" financial difficulty, (b) an acknowledgment that the problem could be resolved by violating trust, (c) the capacity to verbalize or later rationalize the criminal act. This hypothesis later developed into the Fraud Triangle, namely "pressure," "opportunity," and "rationalization."

Pressure

Cressey (1950) originally limited the pressure side of the triangle to a non-shareable financial problem because, he argued, individuals in positions of financial trust also had an obligation to avoid gambling, excessive drinking, and having extramarital affairs in consideration of their social position. However, when these people began indulging in illicit activities, they would start piling up debts, which must be kept secret and, consequently, became a non-shareable financial problem. Rather than seeking help, these individuals violate their trusted positions and commit fraud. Cressey (1953) went on to refine and extend the non-shareable financial problem into six groups: (*a*) *violation of an assigned responsibility, (b) problems stemming from personal setbacks, (c) problems arising from business failures (d) problems resulting from loneliness, (e) problems caused by an incessant desire to achieve high social status, and, finally, (6) problems resulting from poor employee–employer interactions.*

Regarding a violation of an assigned responsibility, Cressey observed that trusted individuals believed that they had to maintain a certain standard and uphold a high reputation in their social and professional gatherings. When they start engaging in illicit activities such as gambling, they do not seek help because they fear losing their social status and their trusted position, i.e., suffering from a vice. Secondly, problems stemming from personal setbacks become non-shareable because people in trusted positions believe that they will lose credibility even though they are aware that other associates could help them, i.e., poor judgment. Thirdly, business failure can be genuine, but it becomes a non-shareable problem that they must resolve themselves, even in an illegal manner. Fourthly, alienation breeds non-shareable problems because people cannot turn to a support network such as friends, to help resolve the issue. Thus far, the problems have been about maintaining status, but an incessant desire to achieve a higher status usually occurs as individuals start living beyond their means, creating a non-shareable problem that must be financed by utilizing fraudulent methods. In the final problem, although the person is in a trusted position, they may resent their employer because they feel underpaid, overworked, or not properly treated; however, they believe they must carry on working. This becomes a non-shareable problem because they cannot share their dissatisfaction with other colleagues, fearing they will lose their trusted position. The problems, individually or collectively, may lead a person to violate their trusted position and seek payback from their company. Lister (2007:63) defined pressure as the "source of heat for the fire."

All the pressure variables result from a "non-shareable" problem by people in a position of financial trust. However, as will be demonstrated later, when the theory was applied to other scenarios or positions, Cressey's understanding of pressure was flawed, and other factors could cause fraudulent behavior, such as an interesting typology by Kassem and Higson (2012), Figure 2.1:

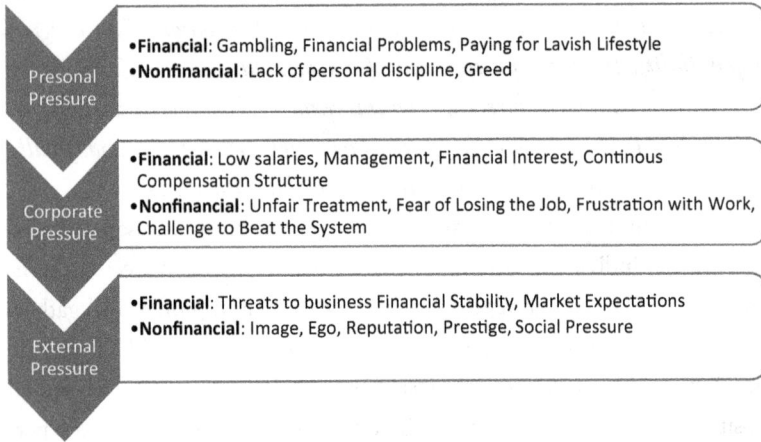

Presonal Pressure	•**Financial**: Gambling, Financial Problems, Paying for Lavish Lifestyle •**Nonfinancial**: Lack of personal discipline, Greed
Corporate Pressure	•**Financial**: Low salaries, Management, Financial Interest, Continous Compensation Structure •**Nonfinancial**: Unfair Treatment, Fear of Losing the Job, Frustration with Work, Challenge to Beat the System
External Pressure	•**Financial**: Threats to business Financial Stability, Market Expectations •**Nonfinancial**: Image, Ego, Reputation, Prestige, Social Pressure

Figure 2.1 Typology of pressure

(Adapted by author)

Opportunity

The second side of the triangle is the opportunity to violate trust. Initially, when the position of trust is obtained, the individual may not perceive any opportunity; however, once the "non-shareable" problem becomes apparent, the trusted person will begin to recognize that there is an opportunity for a resolution, albeit fraudulently. Cressey argued that this shift in perception was based on experience and sources such as associates who engage in fraud or news stories. In addition, these trust violators need to possess the requisite skills and aptitude to commit and hide their fraudulent behavior. It is suggested that the skill set that allows the trust violators to be hired is the same skill set that can be used to commit the fraud. Thus, a classic example is auditors or accountants who are trained to identify and remedy fraud, but when encountering a "non-shareable" problem they use their knowledge to take advantage of the control system, i.e., a loophole, and hide their fraudulent actions. Lister (2007:64) considered that opportunity as the "fuel that keeps the fire going" and that even if a fraudster had a motive, they could not undertake a fraud without opportunity.

In short, opportunity is the view or perception held by fraudsters that (a) trust violations can solve their financial problem, (b) a control weakness has been identified, and (c) the probability of their violation being discovered is low.

Rationalization

The third side of the Fraud Triangle is characterized as rationalization, which is the trust violator's effort to dampen the inner conflict that occurs. This rationalization allows the fraudster to give expression such as "I am borrowing not stealing" or "All people steal when they get into a tight spot" (Cressey, 1953) to their deed, thus allowing them to maneuver internally between the contradiction of the trusted person and abuse of that trust, to resolve their non-shareable problem. According to theorists, this expression allows fraudsters to justify their misdemeanors and stay within their comfort zone. According to Cressey (1953), many of the fraudsters acknowledged that they were committing a crime but denied any wrongdoing, enabling them to preserve their self-respect. Also, many were first-time offenders who believed that they were honest and had got themselves entangled into a problem.

Researchers argue that rationalization can be further divided into denial of (a) responsibility, (b) injury, and (c) victimization. A denial of responsibility is the fraudsters' justification that they are left with no options and that, consequently, blame is transferred to the victims, or denial of any personal benefit, making their fraudulent acts selfless. A denial of injury implies that the harm resulting from their trust violation will not hurt anyone, including people in big organizations, or if they are insured, i.e., moral hazard. Finally, denial of victimization occurs when the fraudsters believe that their victims deserve what they are getting or that their revenge is fully justified. The final type of denial is prevalent in toxic workplaces, and a study highlighted that it was easier for employees to rationalize theft from disagreeable work environments. Lister (2007:64) defined rationalization as "oxygen that keeps the fire burning."

Thus far the constituents of the Fraud Triangle have been discussed namely pressure, opportunity and rationalization which can be shown in Figure 2.2.

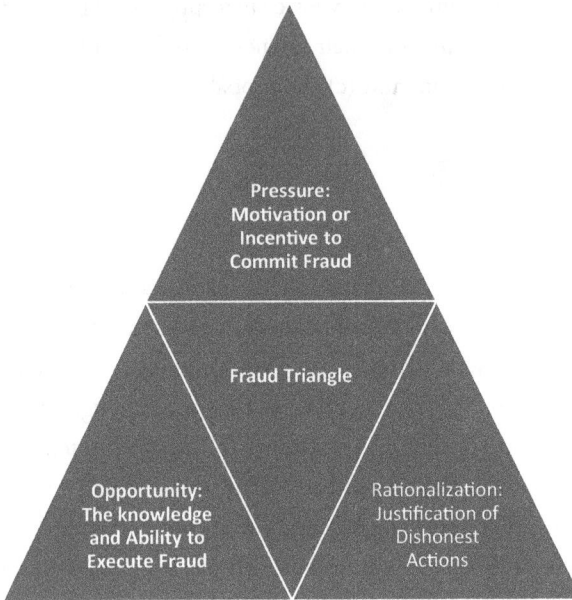

Figure 2.2 "The Fraud Triangle by Donald R. Cressey" (1953)

(Adapted by author)

In 2002 the AICPA incorporated the constituents of the Fraud Triangle into Statement on Auditing Standards 99:

"Three conditions generally are present when fraud occurs. First, management or other employees have an incentive or are under pressure, which provides a reason to commit fraud. Second, circumstances exist…that provide for a fraud to be perpetrated. Third, those involved are able to rationalize committing a fraudulent act" (AICPA, 2002; AU 316.07).

In 2009, the International Auditing and Assurance Standards Board (IAASB) issued an updated version of International Standard on Auditing 240 (ISA 240), which advised that external auditors consider the following three fraud risk factors: pressure to commit accounting fraud, which may exist when management is under pressure from external factors to achieve potentially unrealistic earnings; a key individual may exist who is in a position of trust or has knowledge of internal control deficiencies; and, finally, there may exist a culture that allows for the facilitation and therefore rationalization of fraud. The Fraud Triangle underpins the work of the ACFE.

Evaluation of the Fraud Triangle

The author will now examine literature that appears to support the Fraud Triangle. Loebbecke et al. (1989) developed a model that assessed the probability of significant accounting fraud or management fraud. Their model confirms that for fraud to take place it requires three important variables: motive, "a weak system or opportunity," and fraudsters who can rationalize their actions. According to this model, if any of the latter conditions is missing, it is improbable that accounting fraud will take place.

Researchers created a logistic regression model that predicted the frequency of fraud that supported all three conditions of the Fraud Triangle. This was validated by another academic, who found Fraud Triangle conditions in his sample of fraudulent companies. A robust, 2006, fraud prediction model based on Fraud Triangle conditions, correctly classified fraud and nonfraud approximately 70 percent of the time. The model incorporated factors that were substitutes for pressure, opportunity, and rationalization. However, it was argued that the rationalization variables in the latter study were weak. A similar Taiwanese study found that all their pressure proxy variables for rationalization were linked to a higher probability of accounting fraud. An interesting conceptual study by Choo and Tan (2007) argued that corporate fraud could be better understood by combining the constituents of American Dream Theory (excessive focus on monetary success, exploitation of regulatory protocols, and the rationalization of fraudulent behavior) and the Fraud Triangle (Pressure, Opportunity, and Rationalization).

Albrecht et al. (2008) analyzed the major accounting scandals utilizing the lens of the Fraud Triangle of the past 10 years. They concluded that greed, opportunities such as aggressive applications of GAAP, and, thirdly, rationalization such as a lack of ethics education, were the major reasons for such major accounting frauds. Albrecht et al.'s (2010) study of four major South Korean conglomerates found that they were vulnerable to fraud as per the Fraud Triangle variables of pressure, opportunity, and rationalization.

Before critiquing the individual constituents of the Fraud Triangle, a notable problem with the model is whether it is a general theory of financial crime because it originally studied embezzlers. It is argued that the Fraud Triangle is a *framework* rather than a *fraud theory* and that there is therefore no fraud theory.

Apparently, Albrecht (2014a) coined the phrase "Fraud Triangle," in 1991, when he and his team of researchers conducted a 1979 study in which they generalized Cressey's original model to relate to all types of fraud. The ACFE confirmed that "Dr. Cressey developed the three items (incentive, opportunity, and rationalization), but he did not call it the Fraud Triangle" (cited Huber, 2016). Huber (2016) argues that Cressey agreed to the promotion of the "Fraud Triangle" because it was constructed on his work, and the founder of the ACFE, Dr. Wells, required Cressey's tacit endorsement for the creation of ACFE. Lokanan (2015:202) states that "the Fraud Triangle endorses a body of knowledge that lacks the objective criteria required to adequately address every occurrence of fraud." He suggested that "[t]he ACFE's discourse conceptualizes fraud as a dishonest act perpetuated by an individual for personal enrichment," thus ignoring other influences. He further states that ACFE "perpetuates a discourse that presents a restricted version of fraud. Fraud is a multifaceted phenomenon, whose contextual factors may not fit into a framework. Consequently, the Fraud Triangle should not be seen as a sufficiently reliable model for anti-fraud professionals."

According to Huber (2016), researchers such as Skousen et al. (2009:53) are incorrect in their assertion that the "Cressey (1953) model contends that, to some extent, three conditions are always present when financial statement fraud occurs."

It is contended that the Fraud Triangle lacks empirical rigor and ignores other factors that could contribute to fraud. Thus, for example, Becker (1968), researching from an economic standpoint, argued that a fraudster will weigh up the potential benefits and the costs from punishment, i.e., cost-benefit analysis. It has been highlighted that the fraud triangle is equilateral, implying that each side carries equal credence, but this has not been established to date. Some researchers highlight that the Fraud Triangle is "U.S.-centric" and that until it incorporates societal-level factors such as culture it will remain deficient.

It is maintained that empirical studies using the Fraud Triangle are flawed, although it is acknowledged that it is difficult to undertake this type of research. Rationalization has received little attention and may not "even be observable," and, thirdly, the Fraud Triangle is based on a single criminal, whereas recent frauds such as Enron were executed by multiple actors and that collusion is an important factor in fraud (The last points will be explored in greater detail). Morales et al.'s (2014) critical study on a genealogy of the Fraud Triangle states that it lacks a sound explanation for collusive fraud and has become a professional tool for the ACFE at the expense of "micro-sociological" and "macro-sociological" theories of financial crime. It is argued that the Fraud Triangle ignores group dynamics and other nonfinancial motives such as greed and revenge. An in-depth study by Ramamoorti et al. (2009) of 1,500 executives concluded that "keeping up with the Joneses" was a major motive for fraud. Therefore, non-shareable information is not enough to trigger fraudulent behavior.

Beginning with the pressure side, researchers have argued whether a non-shareable problem is even a necessary facet of fraud and whether theft can be explained by a need for further money. On the opportunity side, it is argued that other nonfinancial variables need to be considered, such as ego and ideology, that force fraudsters to undertake their crimes. It has also been argued that Cressey's model does not consider whether the trust violator has the capability that is necessary to undertake and conceal the fraud. It is suggested that the opportunity to undertake fraud is prevalent in firms that lack a strong corporate governance structure.

Finally, on the rationalization side, it is argued that rationalization is difficult to discern and report and suggested that it should be replaced by "personal integrity," which is easier to study. Other authors state that a major weakness of the Fraud Triangle is pressure and that rationalization cannot be easily observed. Cohen et al. (2010) combined the Fraud Triangle and the Theory of Planned Behavior (TPB), which highlighted personality traits as key fraud risk factors. Their study of words linked with rationalization were found to be more prevalent in fraudulent firms in contrast to a sample of control firms. Murphy and Dacin (2011) created a model that expanded the rationalization side of the Fraud Triangle to incorporate three psychological routes to fraud, namely, poor consciousness, perception in conjunction with rationalization and thinking.

Collectively, these criticisms have led to extensions and updates of the original Fraud Triangle, which will now be examined.

The Triangle of Fraud Action

The Triangle of Fraud Action, also known as the Elements of Fraud (Kranacher et al., 2011), in contrast to the Fraud Triangle, concentrates on the actions of a fraudster rather than the conditions under which fraud occurs. The Triangle of Fraud Action differentiates between the white-collar criminal (whose actions are illustrated by the Fraud Triangle) and the white-collar crime. Rather than opportunity, pressure, and rationalization, the Triangle of Fraud Action comprises of the following observable components, namely, concealment, conversion, and the act.

Concealment is the effort expended to hide the fraudulent act such as "cooking the books" or shredding documentation. Conversion is the method utilized by the criminal to legitimize the fraud, such as overstating receivables to maximize revenue or money laundering. The act is the technique used by the perpetrator to commit the fraud, such as accounting fraud. The Triangle of Fraud Action emphasizes the weak areas in the business rather than the conditions necessary to induce the fraudster. Therefore, it is a useful tool in preventing, detecting, and deterring fraud and consequently makes it difficult for the fraudster to deny the act. It is stated that since all three elements are observable, it is a more robust model of fraud than the Fraud Triangle.

The Fraud Scale

The Fraud Scale was created after a study conducted by the Albrecht et al. (1984), which showed that the Fraud Triangle was a poor predictor of fraud and that it was difficult to profile fraudsters. The Fraud Scale eliminates the rationalization element of the Fraud Triangle and replaces it with personal integrity.

The three features of the Fraud Scale can be modified to assess the probability of the fraud taking place. The scale has two arms: The left arm accommodates great opportunity and low personal integrity; the right arm has low pressure, lesser opportunity, and high personal integrity. If the scale moves to the left, there is a greater probability of fraud occurring because these conditions result in a higher fraud risk; and the opposite is true if the scale tilts to the right. Finally, if someone has a low level of personal integrity, both the probability of rationalization and fraud risk will increase.

MICE

Cressey (1950, 1953) argued that a non-shareable problem was the trigger for fraudulent behavior. However, recent major accounting scandals have demonstrated that fraudsters do not need non-shareable problems to undertake fraud. Dorminey et al. (2012) have highlighted that senior employees who have been convicted of fraud did not suffer from non-shareable problems such as a gambling addiction. It is argued that the major driver of fraud was a high self-image coupled with a competitive culture. Therefore, social status can pressurize an executive to engage in white-collar crime when there is no apparent financial issue.

These observations led to the creation of the MICE (which amplifies the pressure side of the Fraud Triangle). The MICE variables are motivators to commit fraud: M stands for the pressure of money, I is for ideology, C represents coercion, and E is ego or entitlement. The model is considered a framework that can be utilized to understand the motives of fraudsters.

The Fraud Diamond

The Fraud Diamond extended the Fraud Triangle by adding another element, namely, *capability of a fraudster*, which plays a major role in the execution of fraud even if pressure, opportunity, and rationalization is present. Wolfe and Hermanson (2004) argue that the capability is the most important factor when a fraud is committed, because the fraudster has discovered the opportunity to commit the fraud and is convinced that they possess the necessary skills and attitude to successfully execute it.

The six features of a *capable fraudster* are as follows: The person, firstly, has an important position; secondly, the intellectual equipment to undertake the fraud; thirdly, the requisite confidence; fourthly, the ability to intimidate actors to help them undertake the fraud; fifthly, the ability to habitually lie in order to maintain their position; and, finally, resistance to significant levels of stress because fraud can be a complex and drawn-out affair.

The Fraud Pentagon

The Fraud Diamond was further extended by including *arrogance and competence/capability*, resulting in the Crowe Horwarth Fraud Pentagon. It is reasoned that the current business environment in comparison with that of the 1950s has changed significantly. The most notable changes are that corporations are multinational, engage more readily with outsourcing inputs, and employees are subject to performance-based compensation. This creates more pressure for employees, resulting in arrogance or lack of conscience and, consequently, a lack of accountability. Competence is the ability to undertake a fraudulent act by overriding internal and social protocols.

New Fraud Triangle Model

Kassem and Higson (2012) argued that as many factors as possible should be considered when a practitioner such as an auditor is attempting to understand accounting fraud. They proposed the amalgamation of several established fraud models, creating the New Fraud Triangle Model (NFTM):

> Fraud Triangle + Fraud Diamond + Fraud Scale + MICE Model = NFTM

The NFTM incorporates the attributes of *motivation, opportunity, integrity, and capability of the would-be fraudster.*

The A-B-C Model

The A-B-C model was proposed by Ramamoorti et al. (2009) and does not extend the Fraud Triangle. Instead, it focuses on the probability of the fraud under specific circumstances. The A-B-C model is made up of the following: *bad apples or an individual fraudster, bad bushels or collusive fraud, and bad crop or cultural and societal values that can affect the frequency of fraud.*

Predator versus Accidental Fraudsters

Schrand and Zechman (2012) discovered that 75 percent of fraud was committed by individuals who were usually honest, law abiding, and who in normal situations would never attempt to commit a crime, i.e., *The Accidental Fraudster.* This type of fraudster fits the Fraud Triangle. However, some people are predators who continuously break the law, and research suggests that after a first-time offense rationalization becomes much easier, because the perpetrator becomes desensitized and will continue defrauding until apprehended. Therefore, for the predator, the Fraud Triangle collapses into opportunity, while pressure and rationalization change into arrogance and the fraudulent act transforms into a whim or desire. It is believed that predators are well organized and able to mislead auditors with their complex scheming.

The C R I M E Model

The C R I M E model is a fraud model developed by Rezaee (2005), where *"Cooks," "Recipes," "Incentives," "Monitoring," and "End results"* explain the causes and effects of accounting fraud. It highlights the importance of corporate governance and provides novel strategies to prevent accounting fraud. The "cooks" are the perpetrators of accounting fraud, and it was found that in 80 percent of cases either the CFO or CEO was responsible. The "recipes" were the techniques used to execute accounting fraud, and earnings management was the most popular method. The "incentives" were the motivations for committing accounting fraud and are usually understood to be economic but can also encompass psychological and ideological factors. The foremost "monitoring" mechanism is corporate governance. The "end results" of accounting fraud can be substantial, such as company liquidation and delisting from a capital market. The C R I M E model investigated nine cases that resulted in excess of $500 billion of damage.

Nijenhuis (2016) extended the C R I M E framework by adding "S," *which stands for "sentences,"* which were the legal sentences that the fraudsters received, including jail time or fines or community service. It is argued that effective jail sentences prevent fraud.

Motivations for Accounting Fraud

The literature concerning the motivations for management to perpetrate accounting fraud concentrates mainly on pay, attracting and/or maintaining finance, exceeding or upholding market expectations, covering up financial problems or socioeconomic and psychological pressures.

Pay

Senior management remuneration contracts usually cover all or a mixture of share options, cash compensation, including bonuses, and share ownership. Share options allow holders to purchase company shares at an option exercise price that may be, but is not always, below the stock market price. An investigation of recent accounting scandals concluded that the major factor in such unprecedented frauds was exaggerated management compensation. It is argued that executives' pay that is based on options tends to engage in higher risk. It was discovered that senior management of publicly listed companies such as AIG were highly remunerated but made poor judgments, and, in some instances, there was alleged accounting fraud. It is suggested that management can be under immense pressure, especially when company success is directly correlated with their compensation plan, which can make them select accounting policies that may result in accounting fraud. This has also been noted by the Financial Services Authority (2009), who observed that executive pay contracts in British banks can encourage some managers to take unjustified risks that apparently, in the short term, generated exorbitant windfalls but eventually jeopardized the entire banking system. Further studies have found that pay contracts could engender short-termism including profit growth, a high share price, and, ultimately, a higher stock-option value at the expense of shareholder wealth. Hence, when bona fide results no longer support the share price, some managers will resort to accounting misapplication and fraud to maintain the façade of short-term profit growth and stock and option values.

Even where cash is the major constituent of the pay contract, this may still not guarantee or lessen accounting fraud if there is a culture of corruption and management is not concerned with shareholder welfare.

According to Agency Theory, increasing company ownership should diminish a manager's desire to engage in accounting fraud. Therefore, equity-based compensation has become a favored technique to reduce the gap between management and shareholders and expand the value of the company. However, recent frauds, including Enron and post-Enron, have been executed by managers who had material ownership of the company. A sophisticated model was used to investigate managers' equity-based remuneration contracts and discovered that managers will usually deceive the company earlier with stock options rather than with a comparable cash pay package consisting of shares.

On the other hand, it has been reported that higher ownership or equity-based remuneration will not necessarily reduce the propensity to undertake fraud unless the advantage from fraud is completely mitigated via the penalty. Therefore, more managers may engage in a strategy to behave fraudulently when it suits them. An empirical study investigating the link between incentive-based remuneration packages and the probability of accounting fraud established that managers of companies with weak operating performance or results usually commit accounting fraud and have equity-based pay structures. Remunerating nonexecutive directors in the UK context (FRC, 2019) with stock options may weaken their independent oversight and potentially motivate them to misstate financial results.

It has been found that the likelihood of fraud is positively correlated with unlimited share incentives. This was confirmed by a study that investigated the connection between equity-based compensation and the frequency of fraud and found that raising the level of equity-based remuneration results in a higher instance of accounting fraud. This result was further confirmed by a study that established a positive correlation between management stock options and accounting fraud.

In contrast, there are other studies that show that there is no proven link between accounting fraud and pay contracts, although it is important to note that these are from the pre-Enron era. A study evaluated management equity incentives of companies suspected of accounting fraud by the Securities and Exchange Commission (SEC) (1996 to 2003) but could not establish any relationship between accounting fraud and pay. A logistic regression model was created to study if there was a relationship between the probability of accounting fraud and managers' share options and cash remuneration. This study found no correlation between the possibility of fraud and managers' cash compensation and share ownership.

It is apparent from the discussion that prior research on pay, as a determinant of accounting fraud, is at best mixed and that further specific research needs to be conducted, for example, on the type of industry, but this is outside the scope of the current study.

The Need to Obtain Finance

Research suggests that the need to obtain finance can be a trigger for senior management to execute accounting fraud. For example, there may be a need to raise more capital or alternative lines of credit, and accounting fraud may be the only mechanism to achieve these financial goals.

A pre-Enron study established that the key determinant of accounting fraud was the requirement to raise further capital. The need for cheap outside finance, coupled with the requirement to sidestep debt covenant limits, can induce management to maliciously influence earnings. The need to secure higher cash amounts when issuing fresh stock/shares can be a purported reason for management to commit accounting fraud. Senior management may encounter intense pressure to continuously issue suitable results; otherwise external stakeholders may lose confidence or jeopardize access to additional capital. It has been suggested that pending long-term finance, including debt or equity, may be a motive for companies to engage in accounting fraud. It has been determined that if management wants to issue equity at a reasonable cost, they may be more inclined to engage in earnings management.

Exceeding or Upholding Market Expectations

Previous literature indicates that exceeding or maintaining market expectations can potentially motivate management to undertake accounting fraud. For example, it may desire long-term finance from an initial public offering (IPO), achieve corporate objectives, or beat market analysts. It is argued that senior management is aware that not maintaining analysts' forecasts can have a detrimental effect on company share price performance and that thus there is pressure on it to alter earnings through accounting fraud. It has also been reported that listed companies are under intense pressure to issue earnings reports that, at a minimum, meet market expectation rather than maximizing shareholder wealth because senior pay would be jeopardized.

The C R I M E model established that incentives for accounting fraud included upholding market expectations by exaggerating the company results, raising additional cash through an IPO, achieving corporate objectives, and manipulating share prices to raise the demand for issuance of more share capital.

It is contended that improbable, if not unrealistic, Wall Street expectations encourage senior management to execute accounting fraud. It has been established that the desire to meet outside earnings targets causes accounting fraud, especially in the short term. Perols and Lougee (2010) argued that "meet or beat analyst forecasts" are probably forcing companies to commit accounting fraud even when there is no evidence of previous earnings management or accounting fraud.

Covering Up Company Financial Problems

According to an in-depth study involving 200 companies, in 1999, senior management may have undertaken accounting fraud to improve declining results, in order to maintain or increase share prices, avoid delisting, or conceal the fact that company assets were stolen or utilized for personal use. The companies in the study were either experiencing material losses or were close to break-even. This suggests that poor company results may incentivize accounting fraud.

It has been noted that companies experiencing severe financial distress were more likely to commit accounting fraud and that, consequently, external auditors should remain vigilant. This pattern has been established in bankrupt firms, which may be more prone to undertake accounting fraud to cover up financial problems and engage in aggressive earnings management before company failure.

After studying the most notorious accounting scandals of the early 2000s, such as Enron, researchers concluded that the most important motivator to commit accounting fraud was growing debt and the need to conceal it. Further research suggests that senior management who commit accounting fraud are usually attempting to avoid major corrections to the company share price.

A multiple regression model, using a sample of Malaysian companies in 2008 to ascertain the drivers of accounting fraud, found that severe financial problems were the primary variable. A study in 2011 of fraudulent financial statements by listed Chinese companies, using multiple regression analysis, showed that companies used earning management techniques to conceal losses in order to avoid being de-listed from the stock exchange. In the Egyptian context, it was found that the senior management need to maintain, if not exceed, previous financial results was the major motivation to engage in accounting fraud.

Socioeconomic and Psychological Pressures

Researchers agree that personality type is a significant factor that plays a major role in the fraudster profile. For example, a passive person is less likely to engage in fraud than an active person. Anderson and Tirrell's (2004) study suggests that executives are motivated to engage in accounting fraud for the following reasons: excessive or extreme association with the business, a huge ego, familial pressures, company expansion strategies, and concern for company existence. Zahra et al. (2005) took a multidisciplinary approach to their study utilizing the lens of criminology, economics, psychology and sociology, economics, and criminology to establish the likelihood of accounting fraud. They found "socio-level" factors such as "differential association and strain," "industry-level factors" such as culture and values, and "firm-level factors" such as board structure that had an impact on the likelihood of accounting fraud.

Undoubtedly, greed is an important motive for undertaking accounting fraud. Ball (2009) argued that executives whose identity is constructed around the company are prone to commit accounting fraud on account of poor results as a "protective mechanism." Rezaee and Riley (2010) suggest that notions of "self-esteem" can also encourage senior management to engage in accounting fraud.

Psychological factors, including the Dark Triad, will be elaborated by the author after briefly outlining the literature around the prevention, deterrence, and detection of accounting fraud.

Prevention, Deterrence, and Detection

Prevention and deterrence protocols are designed to lessen the opportunity for fraudsters while detection occurs post fraud. It has been argued that when an organization has robust mandates, this sends strong signals to potential internal and external fraudsters. According to Dorminey et al. (2012:573), fraud deterrence works when "(1) the perception of deterrence is present and (2) potential perpetrators recognize that they will be punished when caught."

Studies highlight that the potential fraudsters must believe that detection is highly probable, otherwise fraudulent activities will not lessen. Kranacher et. al. (2011) states that detection comprises of three parts, namely, financial statement audit, focused risk assessment, and examination of management overrides. However, accounting fraud remains a significant concern for the audit profession. Hence, it is vital to create an audit plan that will enable the auditor to discover any deficiencies in the system that may permit fraud. The established methods for helping audit planning are maintenance of a fraud policy, a fraud vulnerability review, an anonymous hotline, and extensive background checks.

It has been suggested that employees should attest to having understood the fraud policy, which should be underpinned with training workshops and periodic reviews. Fraud vulnerability reviews analyze the extent of fraud risk to the company, including location of assets and how they could be stolen. In addition, there should be an anonymous hotline where internal and external stakeholders can report fraudulent activities in a safe space. Unfortunately, personnel files are not adequately maintained, so there should be secondary checks to ensure that initial information supplied at application, such as education or work experience, is correct, as a measure to weed out potential fraudsters.

It is the function of management to create a system of prevention and detection, which is best achieved when compliance systems are at the heart of the business. Schnatterly (2010) argues that if the following conditions are implemented, namely, transparency of policies and procedures, effective communication, and performance-related pay for all employees, then the risk of fraud should fall drastically. However, management override is viewed as the "Achilles heel" of fraud prevention (AICPA, 2005) and results in damaging collusive fraud such as Enron. Therefore, fraud prevention must be instituted at all levels in the organization, including senior management. The detection of management override usually results from anonymous tips, underscoring the importance of an anonymous hotline.

Internal Controls

Accounting information, or, more precisely, financial statements, allow the allocation of scarce resources in an economy underpinned by internal controls, which is associated with the opportunity side of the Fraud Triangle. Hence, even if an opportunity is discovered appropriate internal controls can help detect a fraud.

An internal control is part of a system of internal controls for an organization that is established by senior management, including internal checking, auditing, and other controls that allow the reliable functioning of a business. Nijenhuis (2016) describes five key features that are present in most internal control systems, namely, control environment, risk assessment, control activities, information and communication, and monitoring, which collectively lead to a strong internal control system. The correct application of an internal control system ensures the safeguarding of assets and veracity of records and leads to an efficient and effective control environment. It is argued that an effective internal control system is one of the major steps taken by an entity toward the prevention of fraud.

It has been established that a robust internal control system enhances corporate governance, raises management performance, and dampens fraud, because the entire workforce is involved in the detection of fraud. In contrast, weak internal controls not only lead to fraud but also raise the control risk.

Control risk is the risk of internal controls not preventing or detecting misstatements that provide assurance for an organization's assets and records.

Ethical Culture

Kaptein (2011:846) reminds us that an ethical culture can be defined as "the perception about the conditions that are in place in the organization to comply or not comply with what constitutes unethical and ethical behaviour." An ethical culture in conjunction with sound internal controls ensures a greater degree of prevention. Internal control provides the tools to detect fraud, whereas an ethical culture creates an environment where it is perceived by everyone that fraud is wrong. An ethical culture undermines the rationalization of fraud, as per the Fraud Triangle, as it signals to employees that fraud is erroneous. Ethical business environments provide deterrence, because hiding fraudulent acts will become increasingly challenging and punishment is guaranteed once the fraudster is apprehended.

A CEO should lead by example and create a highly ethical and honest culture that will pay dividends in the long run. A study found a strong correlation between companies that had an ethical culture and stronger performance in comparison with their competitors. Arjoon (2005:349) states that "ethics is truly an essential ingredient for business success," as demonstrated by another study, which suggested that employee commitment increases.

Red Flags of Accounting Fraud

As discussed earlier, all three conditions of the Fraud Triangle, namely pressure, opportunity, and rationalization, must exist before a fraud will potentially take place. Consequently, the key to preventing fraud is breaking the Fraud Triangle.

A red flag is one or more conditions that are abnormal in nature or differ from the norm. It is an indication that something is wrong and should be further investigated. The author will begin with generalities, or what are referred to as *soft red flags,* and move on to specific accounting or what the author regards as *hard red flags*.

Common internal control weaknesses that can operate as red flags include:

- deficient segregation of duties;
- inadequate physical safeguards;
- unsatisfactory independent checks;
- improper authorization of documents and records;
- override of existing controls;
- and a faulty accounting system.

Analytical irregularities are relationships that do not make sense and that appear to be unreasonable. These include large or small transactions that occur at strange times that may involve personnel not normally associated with them. Examples of analytical irregularities include

- company assets sold below market value;
- many bank accounts;
- downsizing in a healthy economy;
- and unexpected overdrafts or shortages of cash.

Operational anomalies are curious events concerning a company's operations. Although they may not be within the control of management, they warrant attention as a red flag for possible fraud. Some of these anomalies are:

- shortage of capital;
- repeated changes in lawyers or seeking multiple expert opinions;
- frequent changes in senior management;
- high staff turnover;
- and significant changes in employee attitude or lifestyle.

Cash being the most commonly stolen asset, accountants should focus attention on the red flags of cash embezzlement and accounts receivable, and these may include

- an unnecessary number of voids;
- discounts, and returns;

- unexpected activity in an inactive bank account;
- customer complaints about notices for defaulting or nonpayment of accounts;
- inconsistencies between bank deposits and deposits posted to the company records;
- an unusual quantity or extent of expense items or reimbursements to staff or senior management;
- unusual cash transactions;
- frequent write-offs of accounts receivable;
- and an increase in the allowance of doubtful accounts.

Payroll is normally an automated or outsourced function that is open to collusion and fraud. Red flags in this area include

- overtime claimed during a quiet period or by staff who would not normally do so;
- negative and material variations between standard and actual wages;
- staff with little or no payroll deductions;
- and "ghost employees."

Purchasing or procurement results in a significant outflow of monies within most companies and is susceptible to fraud. Similarly, an organization's inventory can be vulnerable to theft. Red flags indicating that the procurement and inventory functions are being manipulated include

- a rising number of complaints regarding products or services;
- an increase in the purchasing of inventory but no growth in sales;
- peculiar inventory reduction;
- the proliferation of scrap items and reorders for the same materials;
- and surplus or slow-moving inventory.

As noted in earlier sections, the rationale for manipulating the financial reporting function or engaging in accounting fraud is different from the embezzlement of company assets. Accounting fraud does not result in an explicit financial advantage to one individual. Instead, it supplies an implicit gain in the shape of higher share prices, superior stock options for managers, and continued lines of credit. However, red flags are often present in accounting fraud, just as they are in asset misuse schemes. The following are some of the red flags seen in accounting fraud:

- aggressive revenue recognition;
- extraordinary and profitable transactions toward the end of reporting periods;
- boosting profits by selling undervalued assets or recording one-time events as operating income;
- persistent negative cash flows while reporting positive or growing profits;
- expenses rising quicker than revenues or sales;
- use of misleading classifications;
- capitalizing operating costs;
- pressure to report positive or growing profits;
- material and growing transactions with related parties;
- regularly changing accounting policies such as depreciation technique;
- and using SPEs to improve gearing.

As an early warning system (EWS), the above red flags indicate the potential for accounting fraud. Red flags are a cost-effective EWS that may be used to detect and thwart accounting fraud.

Governmental Regulation

In order to protect the global capital markets from recurring fraud, rules and regulations are required. Moreover, for capital markets to operate efficiently, the quality, reliability, and integrity of financial statements supplied by companies to the market must be true and fair. Therefore, we will briefly explore the Sarbanes–Oxley Act 2002 (SOX-2002), which was instituted in the United States as a response to the menace of accounting fraud.

At the turn of the 21st century, the United States experienced major accounting scandals such as Enron, WorldCom, and Tyco that resulted in severe socioeconomic damage. The table, Table 2.2, highlights the asset size of the top ten bankruptcies to date (Frunza, 2016:394):

Table 2.2 Top ten bankruptcies to date

Rank	Company	Date	Country	Sector	Assets (B$)
1	Lehman	15.09.08	United States	Investment Bank	691
2	Washington Mutual, Inc.	26.08.08	United States	Savings & Loan Holding Co	328
3	WorldCom, Inc.	21.07.02	United States	Telecommunications	104
4	General Motors	6.01.09	United States	Manufactures & Sells Motor Vehicles	91
5	Kaupthing Bank	9.10.08	Iceland	Banking	87
6	CIT Group, Inc.	11.01.09	United States	Banking Holding Co.	80
7	Enron Corp.	12.01.01	United States	Energy Trading, Natural Gas	66
8	Conseco, Inc.	17.12.02	United States	Financial Services Holding Co.	61
9	Chrysler, LLC	30.04.09	United States	Manufactures & Sells Motor Vehicles	39
10	Thornburg Mortgage, Inc.	5.01.09	United States	Residential mortgage	37

This led to growing calls for reform of business practices and accounting standards for listed companies that culminated in SOX-2002. SOX-2002 reporting lists a body of rules and regulations that are designed to align the interests of management and shareholders and reduce the risk of fraudulent activity.

SOX-2002 was supposed to enhance corporate governance of listed companies and, crucially, the confidence of investors in U.S. capital markets. Researchers found that SOX-2002 had improved the quality of financial information supplied to the public and that to a large degree investor confidence in financial reporting and the capital markets had been restored. Hochberg et al. (2014:575) stated that SOX-2002 had "improved disclosure, transparency, and corporate governance, thereby reducing misconduct and mismanagement by insiders, and that for shareholders overall, these benefits may outweigh the costs of compliance." The final point regarding costs of compliance is important because foreign companies may be deterred from entering American capital markets in view of the excessive burden of compliance. Also, it has been observed that post SOX-2002 companies are more careful with their spending.

Dark Triad

Epstein and Ramamoorti (2016) suggest that in the face of the Dark Triad personality types, the Cressey Fraud Triangle collapses into a "single dimension," namely, opportunity. So what is the Dark Triad?

Recent research has highlighted three nonstandard (or deviant) personality types or categories whose behaviors may help to explain accounting fraud. These personality types have been designated narcissism, Machiavellianism, and psychopathy, i.e., the Dark Triad.

Narcissistic people are grandiose, prideful egotists who demonstrate deficient empathy toward others. These individuals are obsessed with power and prestige and are incapable of seeing the damage this causes to themselves and others. The Machiavellian personality is strategic, deeply cynical, inclined toward deception, and utilizes other people to achieve their ambitions. Lastly, the psychopath is short of empathy and will not hesitate to engage in dangerous and reckless behavior. All three personality types share themes of "deceitfulness, self-promotion, coldness, disagreeableness, exploitation and aggression" (Furnham et al., 2013). Psychopathy is considered the most sinister personality trait of the Dark Triad.

Dark Triad CEOs and CFOs

The business world is littered with Dark Triad fraudsters such as "Chainsaw Al Dunlap," CEO of Scott Paper, and, finally, Sunbeam Products, who showed no remorse when making thousands of redundancies and was branded a psychopath. "Crazy" Eddie Antar was a self-confessed psychopath; however, he used this portrayal to gain a reduced sentence for his fraud (Wall Street Journal, 2012). Aaron Beam, a CFO who engineered the HealthSouth's fraud, accused the CEO, Richard Scrushy, of being a psychopath. The notorious Enron CFO, Andrew Fastow, has been characterized as a narcissist.

Research indicates that senior management contain a greater degree of Dark Triad personalities in comparison with society at large. It has been hypothesized that the frequency of psychopaths on Wall Street may be more than 10 percent. Given the high degree of pervasiveness of psychopaths in the business world, Epstein and Ramamoorti (2016) argued that external auditors should incorporate the "Dark Triad personality risk" feature into their formal risk evaluations and protocols. Because auditors remain ill-informed about the potential incidence of such personality types, there is a greater likelihood of accounting fraud.

The Dark Triad helps to explain why some fraudsters are motivated to commit accounting fraud, in contrast to "accidental or situational fraudsters," who yield to pressure when the occasion arises and even these "accidental or situational fraudsters" will eventually normalize their behavior. According to the sociology literature, this is known as the "normalization of deviance" (Vaughn, 1983).

Relevance of Dark Triad to Fraud Prevention and Detection

As discussed earlier, the theory of fraud detection and prevention is normally structured in the shape of the Fraud Triangle (Cressey, 1973). The Fraud Triangle model suggests that three conditions must be present for a fraudulent activity: a motive for the deed, a supposed opportunity to execute the deed, and a standpoint that allows the fraudster to rationalize the deed. It is maintained that with respect to the Dark Triad the psychopathic tendency has a direct effect on rationalization of the Fraud Triangle.

Psychopaths may also impact the other remaining sides of the Fraud Triangle, namely, pressure and opportunity. Internal control mechanisms based on the threat of detection and retribution lower apparent opportunity. On the other hand, psychopaths are usually fearless and self-assured in their capability to maneuver their way out of punishment. The Kranacher et al. (2011) MICE (money, ideology, coercion, and ego or entitlement) model further reveals the pressure side of the triangle. Psychopaths are normally selfish and have a grandiose sense of entitlement that may motivate fraud. Paulhus and Williams (2002) and Babiak and O'Toole (2012) noted that psychopaths are prone to "thrill-seeking" behavior, which may itself be an inducement to commit fraud. According to Bailey (2015), psychopaths "know right from wrong, but do not care."

C R I M E L *Study*

The original research that will currently be undertaken is the use of what is termed as an "explanatory multiple case study" (Scapens, 2004) coupled with an existing fraud model known as C R I M E, as discussed earlier. The explanatory multiple case study approach has been adopted by researchers who want to use real world examples to test the validity of existing theory (Ramus et al., 2003) and potentially extend an existing framework (Van Echtelt et al., 2008). This approach was utilized by Nijenhuis (2016), who investigated internal control failure of a sample of 15 Dutch companies employing and extending the C R I M E to C R I M E S. Nijenhuis also incorporated the victims in **"S"**; however, the author believes that the victims are covered in **"E"**—end results.

The author extended the original **C R I M E model to include "L"— learning, i.e., what is the key learning that we can take away so that we avoid the scourge of accounting fraud?** The author analyzed 33 case studies/companies discussed in the important ACFE-sponsored book, *Financial Statement Case Fraud (2011)*, which was edited by the seasoned and well-respected fraud investigator and commentator, Joseph T. Wells. The industry, whether the CEO and/or the CFO, were involved and if they possessed any psychopathic tendencies, were also highlighted by the author. What follows is a discussion of the key results based on *a typology created by the author. (NB: This is freely available if you contact the author as per the e-mail mentioned in the acknowledgments.)*

The 33 case studies are comprised of a variety of industries, ranging from bioscience to transport, 21 percent of which are concentrated in financial services. Twenty of the case studies are American, and the remainder are international, underscoring the global phenomenon of accounting fraud covering the following countries: Austria, Cyprus, Hong Kong, India, Japan, Jersey, Kenya, Malaysia (two), Saudi Arabia, Spain, UAE, and Venezuela.

It was noted that 82 percent of **"cooks"/perpetrators** were male and the balance female, suggesting that this is a male-dominated crime.

A surprising 94 percent of the offenders demonstrated psychopathic tendencies, such as a charismatic personality, coupled with a desire for absolute control and manipulation. This potentially suggests that global top management is unbalanced and ruthless, which fits the image of the character of the financial fraudster, Gordon Gekko, as played by Michael Douglas in the acclaimed movie *Wall Street*. It is also evident that in a significant number of cases, 42 percent, there was collusion between the CEO and the CFO, suggesting that governance is a real problem, when there is a well-articulated and functioning control environment, because it is subject to management override.

The most favored **"recipes"/methods** of executing the accounting fraud was illegal earnings management, 58 percent, and increasing the value of assets, 33 percent. Illegitimately reducing expenses and liabilities was also utilized. The major **"incentive"** for committing accounting fraud was greed, which occurred as a result of leading a lavish lifestyle. As per Section "Motivations for Accounting Fraud," which explored the motivations for committing accounting fraud, it was found that breaching debt covenants, gaining new lines of credit, and meeting market expectations supported the literature. There were other less known but important motivating factors, such as pressure from the parent company, sale of the business, and a company embarking on an IPO or listing on a public stock exchange such as the NYSE.

As stated earlier, **"monitoring"** becomes redundant where management override is possible, which was present in 45 percent of the case studies. This supports the adage that a ***fish rots from the head down,*** meaning that a corrupt senior leadership is the root cause of an organization's failure and demise caused by accounting fraud. Senior leadership sets the tone and culture for an organization; thus, in 33 percent of the cases there was a poor control culture or willfully poor internal controls. There were several cases showing examples of "control fraud," where the CEO, the CFO, and internal and external auditors all colluded to execute the accounting fraud. In this rare phenomenon, it is practically impossible to detect the fraud until the company implodes. The only solution to detecting and fighting accounting fraud is an anonymous whistleblower hotline. It was also found, in several cases, that external auditors were negligent probably because of poor training or knowledge of the client or industry, which underscores the importance of a quality external audit, although it is not the job of the external auditor to actively search for accounting fraud.

Surprisingly, the **end results** of accounting fraud only resulted in 33 percent of perpetrators going to prison, suggesting that white-collar criminals are not perceived as being as dangerous as other types of criminals. However, as discussed in Section "The Significance and Cost of Accounting Fraud," the socioeconomic costs of accounting fraud are significant and ultimately destroy trust in the capital markets. On the other hand, forensic accountants and fraud examiners require knowledge of accounting, auditing, and investigative skills to conduct an examination into the finances of an individual or business in order to unearth and crucially prove the existence of accounting fraud. Therefore, it is not uncommon for regulators to fine and disbar convicted CFOs from practicing again, as occurred in 15 percent of the sample. In as many as 27 percent of cases, once the crime had been discovered, it was dealt with internally, probably to avoid the reputational damage and the negative impact on external stakeholders such as lenders and investors. This course of action is problematic in that it will not lead to a root and branch clean-up of the culture and implicitly signals that accounting fraud will be tolerated. In some extreme cases, even when the fraud was detected, nothing happened to the criminals, and they were left free to wreak havoc in their next company. Ultimately, accounting fraud is synonymous with corporate failure, as in the notorious case of Enron, and 15 percent of companies studied liquidated after the discovery of the accounting fraud. This can also be viewed as an opportunity for the company to change, as 85 percent of the companies survived and may even have flourished.

The author believes that accounting fraud is a classic case of agency conflict and moral hazard (see Section "Overview of Accounting Fraud," "The Corporate Governance Cosmos"), where inappropriate incentivization, such as excessive bonuses or stock options, perpetuates a culture of short-termism, where the line between "profit making" and "profit taking" becomes very blurred. Hence, in the author's study of 33 international companies, the key strategic **learning themes** gauged were around culture, control environment, and the role of the auditor, as summarized in Table 2.3:

Table 2.3 Key themes from C R I M E L model

Themes	Learning
Culture	An ethical culture must be set at the top
	Long tenure and a position of trust does not clear some of suspicion
	CFOs/CEOs with psychopathic tendencies cannot be treated and need to be removed sooner rather than later, or else the long-term viability of the organization is under serious threat
	Growing or stable dividends are not a signal of a well-run company
	Investors should not be impressed by glossy brochures and the "elder statesman"
Culture	Audit committees and the internal audit function must be completely independent
	Changes in the lifestyle of senior management or junior staff should be considered a potential red flag
	"Control fraud" can and does occur; hence, boards should consider fintech solutions such as blockchain systems that make fraud next to impossible as any changes can be viewed by all participants in the ecosystem
	Simple HR checks can prevent the hiring of incompetent staff, including at senior level
Control environment	There must be a robust system of internal controls to prevent accounting fraud, although these will always be at the mercy of management override
	Wherever economically feasible, there must be a segregation of duties and never too much reliance on one employee, which can be dampened through job rotation, and there should be insistence on the taking of annual leave
Control environment	Board members should be wary of complex structures
	An anonymous whistleblower hotline is a cheap and highly effective tool to detect and deter accounting fraud
Role of the external auditor	The auditor must always remain skeptical and err on the side of caution
	Auditors must keep "management representations" to a minimum
	Auditors should be knowledgeable about the client and the industry, including KPIs, and thoroughly critique "people, processes, and procedures"
	The auditors must undertake in-depth analytical reviews to ascertain any anomalies
	Although it is not the role of the auditor to discover accounting fraud, they should be well versed in forensic accounting techniques, look for patterns or anomalies such as in revenue, and fully understand why journals are prepared

CHAPTER 3

C R I M E L—33
International Stories of Accounting Fraud

The author introduced and summarized the key findings from his C R I M E L model in the last chapter. The author's major contribution is the "Learning" that was garnered through the 33 case studies, and this learning is documented in Table 3.1. This is for the benefit of accountants, auditors, fraud investigators, researchers, and accounting students so that their "fraud brains" are deepened, and they can better detect, prevent, and challenge accounting fraud.

Table 3.1 Complete learnings from 33 case studies

Company Location	Industry	Learning
United States	Transport	Board could have prevented management override of internal controls
		Enhance internal audit function based on learning and CPD
		It was internal auditors who noticed anomalies in doubtful debts after completing forensic accounting course
United States	Construction	Ensure thorough due diligence of company, including background checks of key personnel
		Consider second or third opinion
		Err on the side of caution and liaise with regulatory body such as SEC, early on, to avoid any violations

(continued)

Table 3.1 Continued

Company Location	Industry	Learning
United States	Shipping Logistics	Ensure thorough due diligence of prospective client, including background checks of key personnel Never let a client dictate timelines Never be blackmailed or threatened by a client
United States	Construction	External auditors' overreliance on "management representations" Internal and external stakeholders should maintain a "skeptical" frame of mind "Actual data must be assessed, evaluated" Critique "people, processes, and procedures"
Malaysia	Cosmetics	Requirement for robust internal controls and internal audit function Clear reporting lines Using and promoting forensic tools such as Bedford's Law to detect fraud
Venezuela	Conglomerate	Corrupt company that was run solely for the CEO and his family Shareholders should have challenged CEO long ago but were blinded by continuous and healthy dividends The fraud investigator was very smart to play a cultural card by talking to the press and appearing on a respected TV show. The CEO lost face and was forced to negotiate
India	Transportation	When conducting analytical review, compare against industry standards Consider other ratios such as employee cost to revenue Follow your instincts, even if it means going beyond terms of reference or engagement Maintain professional skepticism
United States	Telecomms	Using a blanket "data preservation order" should set off alarm bells Maintaining professional skepticism
United States	Private Banking/ Financial Engineering	Fine line between profit making and profit taking Although robust internal controls and internal audit function, lack of oversight by parent contributed to fraud Segregation of duties vital Board/stakeholders should be wary of complex structures and audit trails

Table 3.1 Continued

Company Location	Industry	Learning
United States	Credit Union	Lack of segregation of duties Too much reliance on one colleague Encourage staff to take leave Institute CPD, including fraud detection
United States	Conglomerate	Power corrupts Culture sets the tone of the control environment, which must begin at the top and permeate the entire organization Classic example of collusion
United States	Conglomerate	Classic case study of agency conflict and moral hazard, where inappropriate incentivization, namely stock options, perpetuated a culture of short-termism and fraudulent behavior
Not specified	Oil and Gas	Trading floors must have controls and oversight By ignoring the problem, CEO only delayed the inevitable Another case study of agency conflict and moral hazard, where inappropriate incentivization, namely bonuses, perpetuated a culture of short-termism and fraudulent behavior
United States	Brokerage	Be frank and honest with the client, even if it means losing them Carry out all necessary audit testing without interference from the client
United States	Global publishing	This was an example of what I call "Total Fraud," where all major internal and external stakeholders were complicit Perhaps mandatory rotation of senior management is the solution, especially where company stock is used to engender a culture of short- termism and fraud There is little that one can do in such a well-crafted fraud that has gone on for decades SOX reporting forced the issue of outstanding long-term contracts (which required a write-down in equity of $1 billion) that had not been reconciled for years, which if done correctly would take 20 years—this was fudged each year by the auditor. This demonstrates that financial statement fraud will cause time lags and eventually becomes a problem that cannot be hidden

(*continued*)

Table 3.1 Continued

Company Location	Industry	Learning
United States	Leasing	External auditors should follow basic principles such as being prudent and conservative with estimates
		Basic analytical review, including industry KPIs, would have revealed that industry average loan was 9%, while EFCs were 1%—which should have served as a red flag
		Better communication between "origination, documentation and workout" departments would have revealed "double-pledging" sooner
United States	Financial Services	Internal controls must never be sacrificed even for trusted employees—"friendship override"
		Job rotation is a very effective fraud prevention tool
		An anonymous whistleblower telephone line saved the entity further losses, which underscores the effectiveness of this fraud prevention tool
United States	Discounted electronics	Auditors should have maintained professional skepticism and spotted obvious anomalies in revenue recognition
		Audit committees must be independent
		CFO and CAO/Controller should be qualified accountants
Japanese wholly owned subsidiary based in the United States	Auto supplier	Maintenance of professional skepticism at all costs
		Auditing is not enough, and a knowledge of fraud detection techniques is very important
Kenya	Credit Union	Maintenance of professional skepticism at all costs
		Long tenure and a position of trust does not clear someone of suspicion
		Segregation of duties vital in financial institutions, no matter how small
		Change in lifestyle should be considered a potential red flag
Austria	Internet investments	Investors should not be impressed by glossy brochures and "elder statesman"
		Intangible accounting is a highly complex area of accounting, and second opinions from experts should be sought
		Use of graphical methods should be used to analyze trends, especially cash balances

Table 3.1 Continued

Company Location	Industry	Learning
United States	Industrial machinery	Background checks would have revealed that the CEO was a liar —he did not hold a degree as per his CV Fraud Triangle was used as a touchstone throughout the investigation by the fraud examiner
Cyprus	Packaging for FMCG	In this instance, external auditor was very professional and forthright and was not intimidated by senior management Poor operation cycles: revenue, inventory, purchasing, and payroll, result in fraud Situation exacerbated by weak control environment Informal internal contacts can be very helpful
UAE	Charity	Auditors must maintain professional skepticism at all costs Strong internal controls coupled with a robust control environment essential in a charity as it is challenging for not-for-profit organizations to find suitably qualified staff
Jersey	Investment fund taking advantage of forex movements	Fraud examiner should be prepared to look for patterns and categorize information to help investigation There must be segregation of duties Formal reports, including glossy brochures, and even audit reports should be skeptically viewed A successful track record does not guarantee future success
United States	R&D company focusing on life sciences with private and defense contracts	Simple bookkeeping principles such as issuing credit memos to conceal siphoning of revenue and expenses or reclassifying expenses through journal entries to sustain a long-term fraud Auditors must be knowledgeable of bookkeeping and follow-up journals Always undertake due diligence before investing and be professionally skeptical
Saudi Arabia	Conglomerate, but this case study focuses on refrigeration and air- conditioning service	Simple HR checks would have shown that Manager was not qualified, lacked experience, and not fit for purpose Bonus culture generates sales but can lead to short-termism and fraud There should be segregation of duties, especially key roles

(continued)

Table 3.1 *Continued*

Company Location	Industry	Learning
Hong Kong	Sports goods, distribution, and promotion	Culture has a huge impact, and bilingual professionals will be needed to ensure a thorough investigation A weak control environment was the major reason for the fraud Revenue recognition is an important accounting area and should be regularly scrutinized to ensure compliance with GAAP
United States	Electrical contractor	This was a complete fraud Poor control environment Bank should have conducted proper due diligence before extending credit External stakeholders should be wary of awards and personalities as they can be psychopaths
United States	Online company/ start-up	This case study confirms that "Fraud is Rampant" Fraud examiners should follow their gut instincts and document everything to ensure that they do not become the "fall guy" A control environment including segregation of duties needs to be constructed by senior management to prevent and detect fraud
Malaysia	Producing aluminum parts for automobiles	Always undertake due diligence before investing and be professionally skeptical Maintain some sort of accountability mechanisms
Spain	Solar Panels	Basic internal processes were missing such as segregation of duties, code of ethics, and an independent internal audit department External auditors need to maintain professional skepticism and arm's length from client
United States	Construction	Complete thorough audit procedures such as testing of invoices Auditors must maintain professional skepticism at all costs Auditors must understand the industry, including the relevant KPIs

CHAPTER 4

"Cooking the Books"

There are four techniques of executing accounting fraud:

1. **INCREASE INCOME, e.g., premature sales recognition**
2. **DECREASE EXPENSES, e.g., capitalization of interest**
3. **INCREASE ASSETS, e.g., enhance goodwill**
4. **DECREASE LIABILITIES, e.g., off the balance sheet financing**

The following mini-case studies cover these techniques.

Earnings Management

Scott Dalton is the CEO of ABCD Inc. and is reviewing the draft financial statements a month before the year-end.

Income Statement for the Year Ended December 31, 2021

	$
Sales revenue	1,230,000
Less: cost of sales	61,000
Gross profit	369,000
Less: overhead expenses and depreciation expense	345,000
Net income	24,000

Balance Sheet as at December 31, 2021

	$
Assets	
Cash	5,000
Accounts receivable	367,000
Inventory	807,000
Property, plant and equipment	528,000
Total assets	1,707,000
Liabilities and owners' equity	
Accounts payable	451,000
Common stock	1,000,000
Retained earnings	256,000
Total Shareholders' equity	1,256,000
Total liabilities and shareholders' equity	1,707,000

The reported net income is far lower than expected, and Scott directs his CFO to make the following improvements:

A) *Create false sales of $120,000 with a cost of $86,000*
B) *Treat $60,000 of subscription sales in advance as completed sales (with associated cost of sales of $43,000)*
C) *Instruct the sales department to dispatch unordered goods to customers with a sale value of $90,000 (with associated cost of sales of $65,000)*

What is the impact on the financial statements?

1. Sales increase by $270,000 = 120,000 + 60,000 + 90,000
2. Receivables increase by 210,000 = 120,000 + 90,000
3. Payables fall by $60,000 (advance/deferred sales treated as payables before the adjustment)
4. Cost of sales increases by $194,000 = 86,000 + 43,000 + 65,000 (if the fabricated sales are to appear authentic, then the associated costs of sales are recognized)
5. Inventory decreases by $194,000 (representing the goods that have been sold)

The effect of these five changes on the financial statements is as follows:

Income Statement for the Year Ended December 31, 2021

	$	Changes	$	% Change
Sales revenue	1,230,000	+270,000	1,500,000	21.95%
Less: cost of sales	861,000	+194,000	1,055,000	22.53%
Gross profit	369,000	+76,000	455,000	20.59%
Less: overhead expenses and depreciation expense	345,000		345,000	
Net income	24,000	+76,000	100,000	316.67%

Balance Sheet as at December 31, 2021

	$	Changes	$	% Change
Assets				
Cash	5,000		5,000	
Accounts receivable	367,000	+210,000	577,000	57.22%
Inventory	807,000	−194,000	613,000	(24.03%)
Property, plant and equipment	528,000		528,000	
Total assets	1,707,000		1,723,000	
Liabilities and owners' equity				
Accounts payable	451,000	−60,000	391,000	(13.30%)
Common stock	1,000,000		1,000,000	
Retained earnings	256,000	+76,000	332,000	29.69%
Total Shareholders' equity	1,256,000		1,332,000	
Total liabilities and shareholders' equity	1,707,000		1,723,000	

Scott asked his CFO to execute five adjustments, and the effect of three adjustments is highly significant. Net income and retained earnings and, by extension, stockholder's equity have materially risen by $76,000 or 317 percent from the original net income of $24,000, and inventory has fallen by $194,000 or 24 percent.

These changes have considerably improved both profitability and liquidity. However, receivables have increased by 57 percent, which does not improve the company position, although this is theoretically an achievable or realizable asset and payables have improved by 13 percent. **These all highlight the impact of three changes that have a major impact on the financial statements.**

On the other hand, the adjustments constitute accounting fraud. **The first adjustment is blatantly false and will never result in cash flowing into the business in exchange for goods leaving it.**

The **second adjustment** has some legitimacy but does not conform to GAAP, because for sales to be recognized they must be delivered to the customer regardless of when they are paid for. Therefore, until the delivery is made the cash received in advance remains a liability of the company. This accounting entry contravenes GAAP, and the intention is to *deceive.*

On the surface, the third entry appears to be fine because goods have been dispatched and invoices raised. However, no actual orders were made, and some customers will accept the goods and settle the invoices owing to poor internal controls. Although other companies **may return the goods, but after the year-end,** fraudulent sales have indeed been recorded, and again the intent was to deceive.

Manipulating Inventory Valuation

Closing inventory of unsold goods at the year-end is open to fraud because it affects the calculation of profit (as part of the cost of goods sold) and is represented on the balance sheet. Therefore, any increase in the value of inventory will increase the profit, retained profits, and total assets, and vice-versa if there is a fall in the value of inventory.

Inventory valuation is established by comparing the estimated original cost of the goods with their estimated market value and is open to abuse: see the following example. John Rambo is the CFO of HOOVER Inc., which makes parts for the vacuum cleaner industry. John has prepared draft financial statements, as follows, for his board of directors and recognizes that poor profitability will not result in bonus provisions in the employment contracts of senior management.

Income Statement for the Year Ended December 31, 2021

	$
Sales revenue	2,600,000
Less: cost of sales	2,090,000
Gross profit	510,000
Less: overhead expenses and depreciation expense	450,000
Net income	60,000

Balance Sheet as at December 31, 2021

	$
Assets	
Cash	25,000
Accounts receivable	480,000
Inventory	567,000
Property, plant and equipment	774,000
Total assets	**1,846,000**
Liabilities and owners' equity	
Accounts payable	650,000
Common stock	500,000
Retained earnings	696,000
Total Shareholders' equity	1,196,000
Total liabilities and shareholders' equity	**1,846,000**

John is considering increasing the cost of inventory by $100,000 by including manufacturing overhead expense in the definition of cost. The result is the following:

Income Statement for the Year Ended December 31, 2021

	$	Changes	$	% Change
Sales revenue	2,600,000		2,600,000	
Less: cost of sales	2,090,000	−100,000	1,990,000	(4.78%)
Gross profit	510,000		610,000	
Less: overhead expenses and depreciation expense	450,000		450,000	
Net profit	60,000	+100,000	160,000	166.67%

Balance Sheet as at December 31, 2021

	$	Changes	$	% Change
Assets				
Cash	25,000		25,000	
Accounts receivable	480,000		480,000	
Inventory	567,000	+100,000	667,000	17.63%
Property, plant and equipment	774,000		774,000	
Total assets	1,846,000		1,946,000	
Liabilities and owners' equity				
Accounts payable	650,000		650,000	
Common stock	500,000		500,000	
Retained earnings	696,000	+100,000	796,000	14.36%
Total Shareholders' equity	1,196,000		1,296,000	
Total liabilities and shareholders' equity	1,846,000		1,946,000	

Net income, retained profits, and stockholders' equity have all substantially increased by 167 percent from the original net income of $60,000. However, inventory has risen by 18 percent, which does not improve the company position, although this is theoretically a realizable asset. **The company appears to be more profitable and have more assets but all through *smoke and mirrors or fraud*.**

John could also execute the following financial statement fraud to improve the company's profitability. He has the following information regarding the inventory, as per the balance sheet, at the year-end:

Type of Inventory	Cost	Market Value	Balance Sheet
	$	$	$
Raw Materials	100,000	62,000	62,000
Work-in-progress	230,000	155,000	155,000
Finished goods	350,000	392,000	350,000
Total inventory	680,000	609,000	567,000

The inventory of $567,000 has been arrived at by applying the lower of cost or market value rule to each constituent of, for example, raw materials: $100,000 versus $62,000, so choose $62,000. However, if Paul applies this to the total inventory and compares $680,000 with $609,000, then he would choose $609,000, resulting in a $42,000 (609,000–567,000) increase in profits and assets in the financial statements. The GAAP rule has been applied in an alternative method, resulting in an increase in profits from $60,000 to $102,000 ($60,000 + $42,000), albeit in a fraudulent manner.

Fiddling Depreciation Expense

Similar financial shenanigans can be executed in the calculation of depreciation of noncurrent assets such as plant and equipment. For example, the board of directors of FORWARD Inc., a trucking company, is reviewing its draft financial statements for the year ended December 31, 2021, and the reported loss is worrying the board. The company's main asset is its fleet of trucks, and there is a schedule of these trucks and their depreciation for the year. The draft financial statements and accompanying schedule are as follows:

Income Statement for the Year Ended December 31, 2021

	$	$
Sales revenue		2,489,000
Less		
Wages and salaries	875,000	
Truck fuel and maintenance	745,000	
Overhead expenses	533,000	
Depreciation of trucks	400,000	2,553,000
Net loss		64,000

Balance Sheet as at December 31, 2021

	$
Assets	
Cash	125,000
Accounts receivable	321,000
Inventory of fuel	56,000
Trucks	780,000
Total assets	1,282,000
Liabilities and owners' equity	
Accounts payable	185,000
Common stock	500,000
Retained earnings	597,000
Total Shareholders' equity	1,097,000
Total liabilities and shareholders' equity	1,282,000

Depreciation of Truck Schedule—Year to December 31, 2021

Truck	Q.	Cost	Est. Residual Value	Est. Life	2021 Dep'n.	Dep'n to Date	Net Book Value
TA	20	300,000	40,000	3	86,700	173,400	126,600
TB	20	320,000	40,000	3	93,300	186,600	133,400
TC	20	360,000	40,000	3	106,700	106,700	253,300
TD	20	380,000	40,000	3	113,300	113,300	266,700
Total	80	1,360,000	160,000		400,000	580,000	780,000

Depreciation is calculated on a straight-line basis using the net cost (i.e., Cost – depreciation to date) over the estimated life. The annual depreciation is calculated to the nearest $100 in the schedule. **The company's CEO argues that depreciation could be reduced by a minimum of $100,000 because these are estimated figures and turn the loss into a small profit, which would satisfy shareholders.** The CFO is directed to recalculate the depreciation and produces the following updated schedule. **The estimated residual values for trucks TC and TD are increased to $80,000 in each case and their estimated life to 4 years because they were purchased at the start of 2021.**

Truck	Q.	Cost	Est. Residual Value	Est. Life	2021 Dep'n.	Dep'n to Date	Net Book Value
TA	20	300,000	40,000	3	86,700	173,400	126,600
TB	20	320,000	40,000	3	93,300	186,600	133,400
TC	20	360,000	80,000	4	70,000 (w)	70,000	290,000
TD	20	380,000	80,000	4	75,000 (w1)	75,000	305,000
Total	80	1,360,000	240,000		325,000	505,000	855,000

W = (360,000 – 80,000)/4 = 70,000, w1 = (380,000 – 80,000)/4 = 75,000

The impact is as follows:

Income Statement for the Year Ended December 31, 2021

	$	$
Sales		2,489,000
Less		
Wages and salaries	875,000	
Truck fuel and maintenance	745,000	
Overhead expenses	533,000	
Depreciation of trucks	325,000	2,478,000
Net income		11,000

Balance Sheet as at December 31, 2021

	$
Assets	
Cash	125,000
Accounts receivable	321,000
Inventory of fuel	56,000
Trucks	855,000
Total assets	**1,357,000**
Liabilities and owners' equity	
Accounts payable	185,000
Common stock	500,000
Retained earnings	672,000
Total Shareholders' equity	1,172,000
Total liabilities and shareholders' equity	**1,357,000**

The CFO's fraudulent accounting involved manipulating managerial estimates that underpin the calculation. The depreciation method did not change, but the boost to profitability is clearly apparent, from a loss of $64,000 to a profit of $11,000. *Although this is a small profit, it is better than a loss, but the intention is to deceive stockholders and interested stakeholders.*

Dodgy Capitalization of Operating Expenses

A popular technique used by financial fraudsters is to classify operating or trading expenses as capital expenditure. This has the effect of taking expenses from the income statement and allocating them to the balance sheet as a depreciable noncurrent asset. The following example will highlight this phenomenon.

Tahir Qhan is the CEO of Qhan Telecoms Inc., a fast-growing cable operator. The company has been functioning for 15 years, and its cable network has been renewed in several locations during the year ended December 31, 2019. During the year-end there was a major natural disaster, causing significant damage and repairs, costing $25,800,000, which has been accounted for as an operating expense by the company's finance director. The finance director believes this complies with GAAP because the expense is a repair to facilities. The company's engineers estimate that the replacement cable will have an operating life of 10 years. The board is examining the following financial statements:

Income Statement for the Year Ended December 31, 2021

	$	$
Sales		139,800,000
Less		
Maintenance of cable network	37,500,000	
Wages, salaries, and benefits	28,200,000	
Advertising	33,000,000	
Overhead expenses	16,900,000	
Depreciation of cable network	10,000,000	125,600,000
Net income		14,200,000

Balance Sheet as at December 31, 2021

	$
Assets	
Cash	1,200,000
Investments at market value	6,700,000
Accounts receivable	14,000,000
Cable network	78,000,000
Total assets	**99,900,000**
Liabilities and owners' equity	
Accounts payable	8,600,000
Common stock	50,000,000
Retained earnings	41,300,000
Total Shareholders' equity	91,300,000
Total liabilities and shareholders' equity	**99,900,000**

Although the company is recording a net profit of $14.2 million, it is $2 million less than market expectations, and Tahir Qhan is not happy as he and the board will not receive a contractual bonus of $1.6 million. Qhan asks his CFO to redraft the financial statements, showing a much more favorable result:

Income Statement for the Year Ended December 31, 2021

	$	$
Sales		139,800,000
Less		
Maintenance of cable network	11,700,000	
Wages, salaries, and benefits	28,200,000	
Advertising	33,000,000	
Overhead expenses	16,900,000	
Depreciation of cable network	12,600,000	102,400,000
Net income		37,400,000

Balance Sheet as at December 31, 2021

	$
Assets	
Cash	1,200,000
Investments at market value	6,700,000
Accounts receivable	14,000,000
Cable network	101,200,000
Total assets	123,100,000
Liabilities and owners' equity	
Accounts payable	8,600,000
Common stock	50,000,000
Retained earnings	64,500,000
Total Shareholders' equity	114,500,000
Total liabilities and shareholders' equity	123,100,000

The following was done to achieve the redrafted financial statements:

A) Maintenance costs reduced by $25,800,000 from $37,500,000 to $11,700,000

B) Depreciation increased by $2,600,000 (10 percent of $25,800,000) to 12,600,000

C) Cable network increased by $23,200,000 (25,800,000–2,600,000)

D) Increase in net income and retained profits by $23,200,000

This fraudulent financial reporting transformation of the financial statements was all achieved by capitalizing $25,800,000 repairs. **It would be justified to the auditors because company engineers would supply technical reports proving that the repairs were replacement rather than a repair. Tahir Qhan and the board will be satisfied because the results have far exceeded market expectations and triggered their bonus.**

Treating Debt as Revenue Sales

Another way of undertaking financial statement fraud is to engage a willing lawyer to create contracts that hide the **economic substance of the transaction, i.e., they say one thing but mean something else.** The following example will clearly demonstrate this accounting fraud where a company is **seeking additional finance and greater profitability but is already highly leveraged. The solution is to find an approachable bank that is willing to enter into a contract that appears to be a sale but is new debt.**

The latest draft financial statements for BLING!!! Inc. are showing poor results. The board of directors has asked the CFO to explore ways of maximizing profits and generating more funding without increasing already high levels of gearing. The company makes bespoke and expensive watches for celebrities and keeps precious stones for up to 10 years before using them in the manufacturing process.

BLING!!! **has an inventory of jewels whose market value** is $8,000,000, which will not be used for the next 10 years. The **jewels cost** $5,000,000, and their **market value in 10 years is estimated to be** $21,000,000.

An investment bank, BCCJ, has agreed to enter into a **contract where it will buy the jewels for** $8,000,000 and allow Bling!!! to **repurchase them for $17,000,000.**

On the surface this appears to be a **sale, and the contract is written with the legal form of a sale for $8,000,000.** BLING!!!'s records show

- a sale of $8,000,000
- cost of goods sold is $5,000,000

- inventory will also go down by $5,000,000
- a profit of $3,000,000 ($8,000,000 − $5,000,000) is achieved

The crucial point is that debt has not increased when, in substance, this transaction is a loan, because:

- **the $8,000,000 is a loan that will last for 10 years**
- **it will be repaid by the repurchase of the jewels for $17,000,000**
- **therefore, the interest on the loan is $9,000,000 ($17,000,000 − $8,000,000)**
- **(remember that the BCCJ is a bank that makes loans and deposits and does not trade)**

When the precious stones are repurchased they can be used in the manufacture of watches or sold for approximately $21,000,000; thus, BLING!!! will realize another potential profit of $4,000,000 ($21,000,000 − $17,000,000). **This may appear legal, but the intention is to boost profitability without jeopardizing additional gearing.**

Playing with Intangible Assets

Intangible assets such as brands and goodwill are without a tangible physical form but have a significant impact on company's profitability, cash flow, and balance sheet. Typically, accounting standards require intangible assets to be amortized over the useful life of the asset. In practice, many companies write off such acquisitions immediately because of their uncertain value. Current accounting standards allow internally generated intangible assets to be reported. For example, development costs accruing from research and development into new goods and services can be treated as an intangible asset if the project is identifiable, viable, and potentially profitable. However, this practice is open to abuse, as will be highlighted in the following example.

AI PLUS Inc. supply machine learning services to technology companies. AI PLUS has been in business for 10 years and has written off its development costs as operating expenses against revenue. AI PLUS in 2021 made profits of $1,500,000, and in 2021 it incurred development costs of $9,000,000, which were written off. According to in-house experts, only 40 percent of projects, with a useful economic life of 3 years, are ever commercially viable.

The CFO decides to write back the development costs and treat them like a depreciable asset, resulting in

	$
2021 Net income before adjustment	1,500,000
Add: capitalized costs	9,000,000
	10,500,000
Less: annual amortization	3,000,000
Adjusted net income	7,500,000

The profit has increased substantially from $1.5 million to $7.5 million, and the balance sheet will grow by $6,000,000 ($9,000,000–$3,000,000). *On closer inspection, this is a fraudulent transaction because only 40 percent of the $9,000,000 costs should be capitalized, but the CFO will be able to supply venerable engineering reports to the auditors justifying the treatment.*

Technology companies such AI PLUS will be under pressure to capitalize all development costs in the desire that future revenue and profits on viable projects will set off losses on failed projects. *On the other hand, stakeholders will have been deceived regarding the profitability and balance sheet value of the company.*

The Devil's Favorite—Off-Balance Sheet Financing

Off-balance sheet financing is an accounting practice whereby a company does not include a liability or a poorly performing asset on its *balance sheet*. It is used to reduce a company's level of debt and liability. The practice has been severely criticized because it was exposed as a key strategy of the ill-fated energy giant Enron. Off-balance sheet financing is achieved by utilizing a **special purpose vehicle/entity (SPV/E).**

An SPV is usually a strategic partnership between a legitimate reporting company and at least one other entity, i.e., the SPV. The reporting company will usually invest less than 50 percent in the SPV but maintain active control. The SPV's assets, liabilities, and profits are not consolidated into the reporting company's financial statements and are merely disclosed as an investment in an obscure footnote in the annual report. The following is a classic example that illustrates this dubious relationship.

During 2021, ZINC Inc. creates an SPV, called METAL Inc., in which it has a 40 percent investment of $1,000,000. The other investors are BCCJ investment bank and a Gulf-based sovereign fund that both invest $750,000 and hold 30 percent each in METAL Inc.

The CEO and CFO of ZINC Inc. also serve on the board of METAL Inc., and the 40 percent investment of $1,000,000 is funded by transferring nonperforming assets of $3,000,000 and long-term debt of $2,000,000, which is secured by guarantee from ZINC Inc.

The balance sheet of ZINC Inc. before the SPV looked like this:

	$
Profitable assets	9,000,000
Nonperforming assets	3,000,000
Investment in SPV	NIL
Total assets	12,000,000
Liabilities and owners' equity	
Current Liabilities	2,000,000
Long-term debt	4,000,000
Total	6,000,000
Total shareholders' equity	6,000,000
Total liabilities and shareholders' equity	12,000,000

The balance sheet of ZINC Inc. after the SPV looks like this:

	$
Profitable assets	9,000,000
Nonperforming assets	NIL
Investment in SPV	1,000,000
Total assets	10,000,000
Liabilities and owners' equity	
Current Liabilities	2,000,000
Long-term debt	2,000,000
Total	4,000,000
Total stockholders' equity	6,000,000
Total liabilities and shareholders' equity	10,000,000

The creation of the SPV has led to the removal of the nonperforming assets, a lower long-term debt, and, crucially, a less leveraged balance sheet, although it has shrunk by $2,000,000 without jeopardizing equity.

METAL Inc. balance sheet would look like the following:

	$
Cash from investors	1,500,000
ZINC Inc. assets	3,000,000
Total assets	4,500,000
Liabilities and owners' equity	
Long-term debt	2,000,000
Equity	2,500,000
Total liabilities and shareholders' equity	4,500,000

The problem for METAL Inc. is two-fold. Firstly, the ZINC Inc. assets are nonperforming and probably overvalued, thus overstating the assets. Secondly, the ZINC Inc. long-term debt will need to be serviced by ZINC Inc., but the METAL Inc. board will hope that the cash invested by the other investors will be utilized in projects that can service the long-term loan commitments. (N.B. The CEO and CFO are the same for ZINC Inc. and METAL Inc.—clearly a conflict of interest.) However, METAL Inc. will be able to borrow more long-term debt because ZINC Inc. will provide the necessary security.

This is a fraudulent arrangement designed to improve the balance sheet of ZINC Inc., and any cash flows flowing from METAL Inc. would be treated as revenue, thus inflating ZINC Inc.'s revenue, net income, operating cash flows, and cash position. Because ZINC Inc. senior management controls both companies, this may prove to be difficult to audit.

The accounting manipulations discussed in the foregoing case studies are merely the tip of the iceberg and highlight the ease of committing accounting fraud without a deep knowledge of U.S. GAAP or any other accounting standards. Ultimately, it is the intention of the CFO and/or the board and what they are trying to achieve, and the motivations have been discussed extensively in Section "Motivations for Accounting Fraud." In the long run, the only antidote to accounting fraud is a moral touchstone or adherence to an ethical system such as Judaism, Christianity, or Islam, or a stricter law or harsher punishments.

CHAPTER 5

Fintech and the Impact on Accounting Fraud

The author believes that the accountancy profession, especially audit, is set to be disrupted by financial technology (fintech) through the widespread use of Big Data (BD) and adoption of the nascent blockchain (BC) technology. The threats and opportunities from BD and BC will be examined, which will help to ascertain the future of the audit profession and the likely impact on accounting fraud.

Background

The exponential rate of growth of technological development is greatly influencing organizations, especially in the financial services industry, resulting in unparalleled opportunities for improvement and innovation. For example, 74 percent of all banks across the UK expect to eradicate human interaction from their retail banking function within the next decade, and 83 percent acknowledge that they are not supplying the kind of bespoke innovation that digital-savvy customers expect.

Financial innovation can be described as producing and commercializing novel financial instruments/technologies. It takes place in markets and institutions. Cumulative financial innovation, over time, has resulted in the efficient movement of capital and has led to economic growth. Financial innovation can significantly reduce transaction costs, improve security, and potentially lead to superior efficiency. According to a study that utilized data on Italian households' use of debit cards, it suggested that ownership of ATM cards results in benefits worth €17 billion annually to the Italian economy.

On the other hand, fintech delivers disruptive or enhanced innovations to the market, which still utilizes the existing financial infrastructure. The Financial Stability Board (2017) defines fintech as follows : "Fintech is technologically enabled financial innovation that could result in new business models, new applications, new processes, new products, new applications, new processes, new products or new services with associated material effect on financial markets and institutions and the provision of financial services." Therefore, financial innovation does not necessarily require technology, whereas fintech demands the utilization of technology. Comparison can be made between a credit swap, once a significant financial innovation, which necessitated contractual but not technological innovation, and a digital wallet, which is a fintech innovation.

The capacity of cutting-edge technology, such as machine learning, to capture and process large volumes of data in real time, is significantly changing the way business is being conducted. Consequently, new products and services are being created with the consumer at the center, and fintech is confirming this transformation. It is believed that Australian fintech firms have gained a competitive advantage by exploiting digital technologies, which means that consumers enjoy better "price, convenience, access, choice and community."

These changes pose just as many threats to established financial service providers as to the accountancy profession, including the audit and fraud detection profession. "The only thing that is constant is change," a quote from the Greek philosopher Heraclitus, has never appeared truer.

Threat to the Audit and Antifraud Profession

The author believes that the audit profession is poised to be disrupted by fintech. An audit is a statutory examination that leads to an opinion as to the truth and fairness of financial statements. Audit, inter alia, involves the examination of a company's revenues, expenditure, review of the robustness and effectiveness of its systems, and compliance with internal and external controls. The economic context has already changed because the Internet, coupled with the digital transfer of money or cryptocurrencies through distributed ledgers, is potentially altering the way financial audits are executed. BC is the distributed ledger technology that produces an incorruptible ledger of blocks of information that can theoretically be anything from copyright information to financial transactions. Bitcoin was based on an open access model so that anyone can possess a copy of the ledger and change it.

According to analysts, peer-to-peer networking creates new audit challenges because technology has allowed corporations to cultivate *self-auditing and distributed ledgers that are potentially absolute and self-verifying, thus dampening, if not potentially eradicating, the phenomenon of accounting fraud.*

It is argued that that the current model of audit is insufficient to deal with the challenges posed by digital money transfer, storage, and distributed ledger technology. Contemporary audit techniques are not designed to handle the complexity of distributed ledgers, the multiple jurisdiction nature of money/cryptocurrencies, and the time stamping of transactions. According to ISA 200, which deals with the independent auditor's overall responsibilities when conducting an audit of financial statements, audit risk is the risk that the auditor expresses an inappropriate audit opinion when the financial statements are materially misstated, and in a distributed ledger this risk is further heightened.

Companies are producing and analyzing ever more data, including that from alternative sources such as social media. *This allows tech-savvy audit and antifraud professionals to not only consider multiple financial and nonfinancial features of an organization but also provide useful insights, resulting in superior decision-making, better quality audits, and, ultimately, greater value for their clients.* At the heart of these changes is the vast amount of data that the auditors and antifraud professionals need to utilize. The growing volume of multivariate sources of data, which includes audio, visual, text, and video, demand greater storage capacity. Therefore, the author believes that the audit and antifraud profession seems increasingly out of touch in this data/information concentrated, fast-paced environment, making it increasingly challenging for firms to fulfil the needs of their clients, and threatening their very existence in the current form.

Mayer-Schönberger and Cukier (2013) refer to a socioeconomic environment where everything can be recorded, quantified, and captured digitally and turned into data, as "datafication." The result of "datafication" has been the emergence of "Big Data" (BD), a term used to describe large populations of data sets whose size is beyond the scope of regular database software tools to capture, store, manage and analyze. BD is also characterized by specific qualities, termed as the four "Vs," namely, massive volume or size of the database, high velocity of data added on a continuous basis, large variety of data, and the uncertain veracity of data (IBM, 2012). Big Data analytics (BDA) yields immense opportunities for improvement such as a shift away from "data sampling." *Hence, auditors and antifraud professionals would utilize "all" datasets, including those from comparatively messy data sets, and concentrate on correlation rather than causation, creating a major paradigm shift compared with the current audit process.*

As mentioned earlier, BC is a distributed ledger database that keeps a continuously growing list of transactional records arranged into blocks with various safeguards against manipulation and revision. The potential uses of BC are diverse and their effects so far-reaching that some commentators such as Lansiti and Lakhani (2017) have termed it "foundational technology" because it has the potential to produce new foundations for socioeconomic systems and even Internet 2.0" (Tapscott and Tapscott, 2016). It is even argued that in the future, BC technology will lead to complete financial disintermediation.

The threat from BC has been acknowledged by many world-class financial institutions such as BNY Mellon, UBS, and the "Big 4" accounting firms, which are heavily investing in BC-related projects, even start-ups, to stay ahead of the curve and leverage this emergent technology to their benefit rather becoming a casualty of it.

The Likely Impact of BC and BDA on Audit and Accounting Fraud

As BC technology becomes more universal, there will simultaneously be greater opportunities for audit firms and their clients, but the nature of audit and fraud detection will change. In this section those factors that will affect the efficiency and quality of audit or fraud investigation, and the impact on risk assessment and management, will be explored.

External audit and fraud investigations can be lengthy, costly, and inefficient. Auditors and fraud investigators usually spend their time undertaking repetitive and menial tasks that add little or no value to the process.

BC technology ensures the efficiency and reliability of audit by supplying a real-time, auditable log of ordered evidence of events that are immutable and immediately accessible. When a transaction is recorded in the BC and established by subsequent blocks, it becomes a permanent part of the ledger and is accepted as legitimate by all actors in the BC network. This will allow easier and faster audit assurance, which will only increase as the technology improves and becomes more widespread. BC technology should allow auditors to automatically verify or authenticate greater sections of the most sensitive data that underpin the financial statements. All these advances are also beneficial to fraud investigators because they can rely on the BC-based ledger and focus their effort and resources on the actors and relationships in the BC networks as most accounting fraud has an element of management override and collusion.

This would significantly drive the cost and time necessary to undertake an audit and fraud investigation without jeopardizing data security or integrity, because data would be available only to trusted third parties. Many "Big 4" clients use advanced Enterprise Resource Planning systems, thus enabling auditors and fraud investigators to take advantage of BDA capabilities without being forced to develop new skills.

This benefit is enhanced through partnerships between audit firms, financial institutions, IT firms, BD solutions companies, and BC initiatives. The following collaborations between the audit profession and stakeholders such as IT companies (e.g., Hyperledger Project and Data Alliance Collaborative) have resulted in reliable analytical tools and open-source BC frameworks that will reduce costs.

The quality of audit and fraud investigations can be enhanced through BC technology and BDA in several ways. Current audit analytical methods occasionally produce a large number of false positive results that cannot be physically investigated by auditors owing to information overload. However, BDA techniques can significantly reduce the number of false positive results because they identify anomalies and exceptions, along with better systems of ranking, which would also be useful to fraud investigators. BDA will allow auditors and fraud investigators to look at entire data populations rather than relying on small sample sizes. The data/transactions recorded in BC technology are indelible, thereby minimizing the risk of error and preventing data redundancy. In a BC system the integrity of data can be proven rapidly and simply.

It is important to note that the BC and BDA techniques will not dampen the auditor's or fraud investigator's use of professional judgment and professional skepticism. Instead, an auditor and fraud investigator will be able to acquire a multifaceted understanding of the financial reporting system, which should heighten the quality of work and create value for the client.

Business risk assessment (of the client) has always been a most important part of the audit process and any fraud investigation. Thus, 60 percent of participants in a 2017 study believe that audits should ascertain the client's business risks. The use of BDA allows auditors and fraud investigators to study large data sets more effectively and efficiently, which informs the risk assessment undertaken during the early stages of the audit or investigation, allowing effective planning, especially audit planning. It is argued that it is important to exceed minimum compliance standards, and BDA can make this possible. BC technology is particularly attractive for risk management and compliance when multiple jurisdictions are involved.

Cao et al. (2015) highlight the following areas that will be positively impacted by BDA and BC technology, namely, identifying and ascertaining risks connected with accepting or progressing an audit or fraud investigation engagement; detecting and assessing the risks of material misstatement resulting from accounting fraud; identifying and considering the risks of material misstatement by understanding the organization, including its internal controls; executing substantive analytical techniques based on the auditor's assessment of the risks of material misstatement and undertaking analytical techniques toward the end of the audit to help the auditor form an overall opinion or the fraud investigator being more confident in their investigation and findings. Therefore, BDA coupled with BC technology gives the auditor and a fraud investigator a more comprehensive picture of the financial reporting system based on bigger data sets and extensive testing in comparison with current practices.

The Risks of BC and BDA

As already noted, companies are processing huge amounts of BD in terms of volume, velocity, variety, and veracity. However, the seemingly endless data from multiple sources can be of little credible use and unconnected. Therefore, auditors and fraud investigators need to have a concrete understanding of the data they are analyzing and investigating. Zhang et al. (2015) indicate potential data gaps resulting in the use of BDA, data consistency, data integrity, data identification, data aggregation, and data confidentiality. These data gaps can cause many audit challenges, for example, auditing data with diverse formats or the identity of actors in the BC network.

Analysis of high-volume data sets can result in a large number of outliers for which the auditor or fraud investigator may not have the requisite skills, time, or budget to fully investigate. Another urgent problem is the appropriate identification and adoption of BDA tools. This problem is compounded by the fact that auditors or investigators may not possess the necessary IT skills to analyze BD. This is forcing firms to significantly invest in the right BDA and attract and retain the best talent. Any operational savings accruing from BDA and BC technology will be offset by higher training costs or investing in data scientists.

Notwithstanding the assurance of unalterable, consistent, and distributed databases, BC technology faces specific data risks. Although consistency is ensured by the distributed ledger, this creates an expense every time it becomes necessary for a record to be checked with every other record to ensure it is unique, significantly increasing the time necessary to reach an agreement and corroborate the transaction.

In a BD world, security and privacy of data from multiple sources received from clients become even more important because a leak can spread almost instantaneously. Organizations that upload their data to a BC system or even the cloud are exposed to an unknown or untrustworthy environment, making cybersecurity a major issue. The BC system is highly complex, and because audit/fraud investigation firms lack IT/IS/Data Science expertise, they are reliant on BDA and BC third-party vendor solutions, exacerbating security and privacy concerns.

The provision of strong data encryption and supply of public and private keys is one possible solution for security issues in the BC system. However, this creates another challenge, namely, the loss of private keys. Another significant security risk is the phenomenon of "double spending" that occurs when the data in the BC system has been compromised, which increases the chances of further breaches of security.

Although International Standards on Audit state audit practices and there are Computer Assisted Audit Techniques, there is currently no framework for BDA or BC. This highlights the lack of standards or examples of good practice to which auditors or investigators can refer. This will become problematic as different BC systems are created and BDA becomes the norm, leading to protocol problems. Consequently, without a robust framework, auditors and fraud investigators are heading into a professional minefield for which they are generally ill-equipped. Auditors will be unable to substantiate their judgments and techniques performed during the audit process. There is also a high risk that ISAs do not adequately respond to rapid, constant technological enhancements (IAASB, 2016). In particular, the audit of BC technology has received little, if any, attention from audit regulators except a preliminary collaboration between Digital Asset Holdings, a BC-related start-up, and the Australian Securities Exchange (Digital Asset, 2016). Moreover, 66 percent of respondents in a 2017 survey comprising chief executive officers, chief financial officers, and chief audit officers of big companies contended that the biggest challenge to enhancing the impact of audit is the regulatory environment. This means for fraud investigators that they will be operating in highly complex systems that will continue to upgrade because of continuous advances in artificial intelligence and quantum computing.

Other threats stemming from the use of advanced technologies are overreliance on data collecting and data analysis software solutions, overconfidence in the results of the performed data analysis and, consequently, development of confirmation bias, which negatively affects professional judgment and professional skepticism.

In the new BC- and BDA-driven world, it is acknowledged that even testing 100 percent of a data population does not suggest that an auditor is able to supply more than a reasonable opinion. In contrast, fraud investigators will be forced to contend with the potential for real-time accounting fraud and false red flags owing to copious amounts of data.

A 2017 study found that approximately 80 percent of interviewed respondents believed that auditors should utilize higher population samples, and 78 percent believed that auditors should use more cutting-edge IT for data gathering, which is also applicable to fraud investigators. Brown-Liburd et al. (2015) indicated the limitations regarding the processing of information in a BD context, such as information overload and information relevance. In a BDA environment, information can be unstructured, resulting in poor judgments. Another damaging effect of large amounts of data is the tendency of auditors not to ignore irrelevant information. A dangerous effect known as the "dilution effect" can arise whereby higher levels of irrelevant information have been shown to dampen decision makers' ability to identify relevant information (Hodge and Reid, 1971; Well, 1971). The "dilution effect" is particularly relevant in an audit context, because auditors must choose which items are more important for their audit judgments from a large spectrum of information that is equally important to fraud investigators even if they are targeting one area of a financial statement. Therefore, in a BD and BC world, this becomes even more problematic, and auditors and investigators uncomfortable with the multivariate or unstructured nature of BD may avoid ambiguous information, which may result in poor audit opinions or incomplete/flawed investigations.

Responding to the Challenges of BC and BDA

A greater adoption of BDA and BC technology will potentially change both auditing and the fraud investigation profession. It is believed that not only will audit techniques (including fraud investigation techniques) become automated but their scope will widen, resulting in the shortening of professional assignments, and this will ultimately improve the general assurance quality. BDA will probably reduce costs and improve profitability with respect to external auditors/fraud investigators, or cost effectiveness in the case of internal auditors.

The author believes that a paradigm shift is occurring in audit and fraud investigation because, as Dai and Vasarhelyi (2016) suggest, BC or

"Mirror World" technologies can facilitate either individual business processes or the entire value chain and can be digitally represented to ensure control and analysis, as demonstrated by projects such as the Hyperledger Project. This system would enable auditors or investigators to use information in the "Mirror World" rather than, for example, conducting a physical inventory inspection and supplying sequential integrity assurance. As the "Mirror World" or BC system documents the details of business activities occurring in the physical world, it can potentially serve as an independent, if not unbiased, information resource to authenticate the veracity of accounting records.

The effective utilization of BDA and BC in audit and fraud investigation requires professionals to improve their skills. In fact, a significant proportion of today's auditors and fraud investigators will need to reskill in order to fully realize the potential of these technologies. In a 2017 study, the participants stressed the need for auditors to not only be fully conversant with new technologies but also remain ahead of the changes, as will fraud investigators. Furthermore, clients are looking for high information technology/information systems skills, superior interpersonal skills, and critical thinking skills from their auditors and, especially, fraud investigators, who will need to liaise with actors in the BC network. In this regard, PricewaterhouseCoopers LLP, one of the "Big 4" global audit firms that have supported various blockchain projects, has announced (CCN, 2018) a blockchain audit service, which it claims will encourage people to use the nascent technology.

Accounting thinkers caution that with the increased use of BDA and BC auditing, standards must tackle BD, because the concept of materiality needs to be reevaluated and the processes producing this data must be constantly improved. However, it is argued that BC technology can help lessen the disparity between U.S. GAAP and International Financial Reporting Standards (IFRS), eventually leading to a global set of accounting standards that will ultimately dampen accounting fraud. The author believes continuous improvements in BDA, BC, and AI will lessen the gap between relevant and irrelevant data, which has already been achieved in econometrics through "data cleaning."

As discussed, the promised benefits and challenges that accrue from the use of BDA and BC technology in audit, fraud investigation, and, crucially, prevention, are far-reaching if not groundbreaking. However, all important stakeholders, including legislators, regulators, professional bodies, businesses, and IT developers, need to collaborate if these nascent technologies are to become established in the fabric of global business. It is more than likely that if there is no coherent plan then the business world will witness a breakdown of trust between the audit profession and business, resulting in the unthinkable death of audit and irrelevance of fraud investigation focusing on accounting fraud.

CHAPTER 6

Conclusion

Society has bestowed on professional accountants the sole rights to undertake specific services (e.g., preparing and signing off financial statements or auditing them) and rightly expects something in return. Thus, accountants have a major responsibility to maintain the public interest above and beyond their own personal interests. During their work accountants will undoubtedly be confronted by severe tension, as highlighted in Section "Accounting Scandals," as they attempt to balance the conflicting demands between commercial interests, such as maintaining a consistent, if not growing, share price, and their duty to uphold the public good.

This tension will exacerbate during times of crisis, as discussed in Section "Motivations for Accounting Fraud," or, more recently, during the COVID-19 pandemic, which severely disrupted global trade and commerce. These incidents result in ethical dilemmas for accountants, including pressure to engage in accounting fraud, as shown in the chapter "Cooking the Books," or ignore money laundering, ignore profiteering, and make fraudulent claims from various government-backed schemes, such as business research and development grants and assistance with employee furloughed payroll, to help businesses.

So, what is a professional accountant or accounting student supposed to do?

All reputable professional accountancy bodies such as ACCA or AICPA or ICAS expect their members to strictly follow ethical principles. The restructured International *Code of Ethics for Professional Accountants (including International Independence Standards)* (2019), issued by the International Federation of Accountants (IFAC), has established a conceptual framework for all professional accountants to confirm compliance with the following five fundamental principles of ethics:

A) **"Integrity;**

A professional accountant should be straightforward and honest in all professional and business relationships

B) **Objectivity;**

A professional accountant should not allow bias, conflict of interest or undue influence of others

C) **Professional Competence and Due Care;**

A professional accountant has a continuing duty to maintain professional knowledge and skill at the level required to ensure that a client or employer receives competent professional services based on current developments in practice, legislation, and techniques. A professional accountant should act diligently and in accordance with applicable technical and professional standards when providing professional services.

D) **Confidentiality;**

A professional accountant should respect the confidentiality of information acquired as a result of professional and business relationships and should not disclose any such information to third parties without proper and specific authority unless there is a legal or professional right or duty to disclose. Confidential information acquired as a result of professional and business relationships should not be used for the personal advantage of the professional accountant or third parties.

E) **Professional Behaviour.**

A professional accountant should comply with the relevant laws and regulations and should avoid any action that discredits the profession."

In addition, recognized professional accountancy bodies adhere to the IFAC (2019) conceptual framework that requires a professional accountant to *"identify, evaluate and address threats to compliance with the fundamental principles,"* which has been called the **IFAC Ethical Triangle (Sheikh, 2020), see Figure 6.1:**

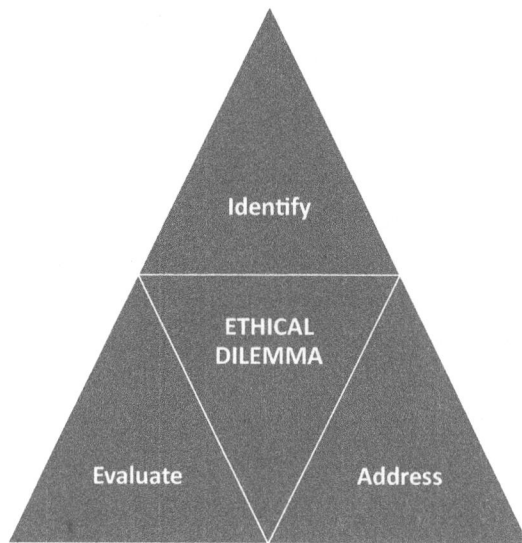

Figure 6.1 "IFAC ethical triangle"

Utilizing a principles-based method to analyze ethical dilemmas means accountants cannot rely on detailed rules, because it is not possible for rules to tackle the sheer complexity of the real world. The great philosopher Wittgenstein (1953) supplies another reason for not strictly adhering to the rules. He argues that rules cannot encompass all scenarios, because they originate in scenarios where specific assumptions are taken for granted but not made clear in the rules. Therefore, when the rules are applied to a fresh scenario, they cannot provide any guidance.

Consequently, ethical issues are usually formulated in the shape of higher-order principles that offer enough flexibility to deal with new and arising situations, such as the economic depression following the COVID-19 pandemic.

The author believes professional accountants will be forced to exercise and take responsibility for their own personal judgments. Indeed, this can be a tough call, for example, when a debt covenant is about to be violated. The IFAC Code of Ethics offers a helpful checklist approach to the resolution of ethical conflict, but, again, this checklist approach is merely a guide:

A) **"Relevant facts;**
B) **Ethical issues involved;**
C) **Fundamental principles related to the matter in question;**
D) **Established internal procedures;**
E) **Alternative courses of action."**

As outlined in Chapter 5, Fintech may be the way forward to dampen the menace of accounting fraud because it can lessen the human dimension through advances in artificial intelligence (AI) or highlight patterns that demonstrate financial statement shenanigans. However, the author believes the human dimension will remain problematic because there is a skills gap that is being addressed by technical education and continuing professional education (CPD). According to the author, the future accountant will be a

Data Scientist + "Storyteller" = ACCOUNTING ENGINEER

However, as people will always write the software code and interpret the data or tell the "story," human intention and action will remain the pain and the cure of accounting fraud.

In short, the following advice from the 3,000-year-old philosopher Socrates; the 13th century poet Rumi; and the medieval father of accounting, Fra Luca Pacioli, can help accountants maintain high ethical standards and not engage in accounting fraud even when they are under immense pressure:

"Regard your good name as the richest jewel you can possibly be possessed of - for credit is like fire; when once you have kindled it you may easily preserve it, but if you once extinguish it, you will find it an arduous task to rekindle it again. The way to gain a good reputation is to endeavour to be what you desire to appear." ~ Socrates

"Run from what's comfortable. Forget safety. Live where you fear to live. Destroy your reputation. Be notorious. I have tried prudent planning long enough. From now on I'll be mad." ~ Rumi

"...never record as a debtor or creditor someone who has not consented...keep your records this way...and get a reputation for false records." ~ Luca Pacioli

Bibliography

Abrams, M.D., S. Jajodia, and H.J. Podell. 1995. *Information Security: An Integrated Collection of Essays.* Los Alamitos, CA: IEEE Computer Society Press.

ACCA. 2017. "Auditors Get to Grips with New Challenges." http://www.accaglobal.com/uk/en/member/member/accounting business/2017/01/insights/audit-challenges.html, (accessed December 22, 2017).

ACFE. 2014. "Report to the Nations on Occupational Fraud and Abuse," *Global Fraud Study.* http://www.acfe.com, (accessed January 1, 2019).

ACFE. 2016. "Report to the Nations on Occupational Fraud and Abuse," *Global Fraud Study.* http://www.acfe.com, (accessed January 1, 2019).

ACFE. 2018. "Report to the Nations on Occupational Fraud and Abuse," *Global Fraud Study.* http://www.acfe.com, (accessed February 1, 2020).

Aghghaleh, S.F., M.T. Iskandar, and Z.M. Mohamed. 2014. "Fraud Risk Factors of Fraud Triangle and the Likelihood of Fraud Occurrence: Evidence from Malaysia." *Information Management & Business Review* 6, no. 1, pp. 1-7.

AICPA. 2002. "Consideration of Fraud in a Financial Statement Audit." *Statement on Auditing Standards* 99.

AICPA. 2005. *Management Override of Internal Controls: The Achilles' Heel of Fraud Prevention.* New York: AICPA.

Albrecht, C., C.C. Albrecht, and S. Dolan. 2007. "Financial Fraud: The How and Why." *European Business Forum* 29, pp. 34-39.

Albrecht, C., C. Turnbull, Y. Zhang, and C.J. Skousen. 2010. "The Relationship Between South Korean Chaebols and Fraud." *Managerial Auditing Journal* 33, no. 3, pp. 257-68.

Albrecht, S., K. Howe, and M. Romney. 1984. "Deterring Fraud: The Internal Auditor's Perspective." *Institute of Internal Auditors Research Foundation* 3, no. 3, pp. 1-42.

Albrecht, W.S. 2006. *Fraudulent Financial Transactions.* PhD Thesis. Brigham: Brigham Young University. http://www.aicpa.org/Pages/default.aspx, (accessed March 1, 2019).

Albrecht, W.S. May/June 2014a. "My Reflections on How the ACFE Began." *Fraud Magazine.*

Albrecht, W.S. July/August 2014b. "Iconic Fraud Triangle Endures: Metaphor Diagram Helps Everybody Understand Fraud." *Fraud Magazine.* https://www.fraud-magazine.com/article.aspx?id=4294983342 (accessed April 2019)

Albrecht, W.S., and C.C. Albrecht. 2002. "Root Out Financial Deception." *Journal of Accountancy* 193, no. 4, pp. 30-36.

Albrecht, W.S., G. Wernz, and T. Williams. 1995. *Fraud: Bringing Light to the Dark Side of Business.* 1st ed. New York: McGraw-Hill.

Albrecht, W.S., C.C. Albrecht, and C.O. Albrecht. 2004. "Fraud and Corporate Executives: Agency, Stewardship and Broken Trust." *Journal of Forensic Accounting* 5, no. 1, pp. 109-30.

Albrecht, W.S., C. Albrecht, and C.C. Albrecht. 2008. "Current Trends in Fraud and Its Detection." *Information Security Journal: A Global Perspective* 17, no. 1, pp. 2-12.

Alles, M.G. 2015. "Drivers of the Use and Facilitators and Obstacles of the Evolution of Big Data by the Audit Profession." *Accounting Horizons* 29, no. 2, pp. 439-49.

Alleyne, P., and M. Howard. 2005. "An Exploratory Study of Auditors' Responsibility for Fraud Detection in Barbados." *Managerial Auditing Journal* 20, no. 1. www.emerald.com, (accessed December 20, 2017).

Alvarez, F., and L. Lippi. 2009. "Financial Innovation and the Transactions Demand for Cash." *Econometrica* 77, pp. 363-402.

American Institute of Certified Public Accountants (AICPA). 2007. "Concealed Liabilities," www.aicpa.org, (accessed January 1, 2019).

Anand, V., B.E. Ashforth, and M. Joshi. 2004. "Business as Usual: The Acceptance and Perpetuation of Corruption in Organizations." *The Academy of Management Executive* 18, no. 2, pp. 39-53.

Anderson, J.R., and M. Tirrell. 2004. "Too Good to be True: CEOs and Financial Reporting Fraud." *Consulting Psychology Journal: Practice and Research* 56, pp. 35-43.

Arjoon, S. 2005. "Corporate Governance: An Ethical Perspective." *Journal of Business Ethics* 61, no. 4, pp. 343-52.

Association of Certified Fraud Examiners (ACFE). 2002. "Consideration of Fraud in a Financial Statement Audit sec.316.35." https://pcaobus.org/Standards/Archived/PreReorgStandards/Pages/AU316.aspx.

Association of Chartered Certified Accountants. 2015. "Why the Audit Profession MustEvolveorDie." www.accaglobal.com/uk/en/member/member/accounting-business/insights/audit-evolution.html, (accessed January 1, 2019).

Azadinamin, A. 2013. "The Bankruptcy of Lehman Brothers: Causes of Failures & Recommendations Going Forward," *Social Science Research.* https://www.researchgate.net/publication/230687440_The_Bankruptcy_of_Lehman_Brothers_Causes_of_Failure_Recommendations_Going_Forward, (accessed March 31, 2018).

Babiak, P., and M.E. O'Toole. November 2012. "The Corporate Psychopath," *FBI Law Enforcement Bulletin.* http://www.fbi.gov/stats services/publications/

lawenforcement-bulletin/november-2012/the-corporate-psychopath, (accessed December 26, 2017).

Babiak, P., C.S. Neumann, and R.D. Hare. 2010. "Corporate Psychopathy: Talking the Walk." *Behavioural Sciences and the Law* 28, pp. 174-93.

Bailey, C. 2015. "Psychopathy and Accounting Students' Attitudes towards Unethical Professional Practices." https://ssrn.com/abstract=2279976.

Bailey, C. 2017. "Psychopathy and Accounting Students' Attitudes towards Unethical Professional Practices." *Journal of Accounting Education* 41, pp. 15-32.

Ball, R. 2009. "Market and Political/Regulatory Perspectives on the Recent Accounting Scandals." *Journal of Accounting Research* 47, no. 2, pp. 277-323.

Baofu, P. 2014. *The Future of Post Human Accounting: Towards a New Theory of Addition and Subtraction in Information Management.* Charlotte, NC: IAP.

Bart Baesens, B., V. Van Vlasselaer, and W. Verbeke. 2015. *Fraud Analytics Using Descriptive, Predictive, and Social Network Techniques: A Guide to Data Science for Fraud Detection.* Hoboken, NJ: Wiley.

BBC. 2003. "Parmalat in Bankruptcy Protection." http://news.bbc.co.uk/1/hi/business/3345735.stm, (accessed November 16, 2018).

BBC. 2004. "New Detention in Parmalat Probe." http://news.bbc.co.uk/2/hi/business/3487192.stm, (accessed November 22, 2018).

Beasley, M. 1999. "An Empirical Analysis of the Relationship between the Board of Directors' Composition and Financial Statement Fraud." *The Accounting Review* 71, no. 4, pp. 443-65.

Beasley, M.S., J.V. Carcello, and D.R. Hermanson. 1999. "Fraudulent Financial Reporting: 1987-1997, An Analysis of U.S. Public Companies," *Committee of Sponsored Organisations of the Treadway Commission.* www.coso.org, (accessed January 1, 2019).

Beasley, M.S., V.J. Carcello, and D.R. Hermanson. 2000. "Preventing Fraudulent Financial Reporting." *The CPA Journal* 70, no. 12, pp. 15-21.

Beasley, M.S., J.V. Carcello, D.R. Hermanson, and T.L. Neal. 2010. "Fraudulent Financial Reporting 1998-2007: An Analysis of U.S. Public Companies," *Committee of Sponsored Organisations of the Treadway Commission.* www.coso.org, (accessed March 1, 2019).

Becker, G.S. 1968. "Crime and Punishment; An Economic Approach." *Journal of Political Economy* 76, pp. 169-217.

Bell, T.B., and J.V. Carcello. 2000. "A Decision Aid for Assessing the Likelihood of Fraudulent Financial Reporting." *Auditing: A Journal of Practice and Theory* 19, no. 1, pp. 169-84.

Benson, M.L., and S.S. Simpson. 2014. *Understanding White-Collar Crime: An Opportunity Perspective.* Criminology and Justice Studies. Routledge: Taylor & Francis.

Biegelman, M.T., and J.T. Bartow 2012. *Executive Roadmap to Fraud Prevention and Internal Control: Creating a Culture of Compliance*. 2nd ed. Hooken, NJ: John Wiley & Sons.

Bierstaker, J.L., G.R. Brody, and C. Pacini. 2006. "Accountants' Perceptions Regarding Fraud Detection and Prevention Methods." *Managerial Auditing Journal* 21, no. 5, 520-35.

Blay, A.D. 2005. "Independence Threats, Litigation Risk, and the Auditor's Decision Process." *Contemporary Accounting Research* 22, pp. 759-89.

Bloomberg. 2004. "Bloomberg Businessweek." http://www.bloomberg.com/news/articles/2004-01-11/how-parmalat-went-sour, (accessed January 1, 2019).

Bowen, P. 2017. "Big UK Banks Racing Each Other to Cut Out All Human Interaction from Retail Banking." https://ibsintelligence.com/uncategorized, (accessed April 19, 2018).

Boyle, D., B. Carpenter, and D. Hermanson, 2012. "CEOs, CFOs, and Accounting Fraud." *The CPA Journal* 82, no. 1, pp. 62-65.

Braithwaite, J. 1984. *Corporate Crime in the Pharmaceutical Industry*. London: Routledge & Kegan Paul.

Brazel, J.F., K.L. Jones, and D.F. Prawitt. 2014. "Auditors' Reactions to Inconsistencies between Financial and Non Financial Measures: The Interactive Effects of Fraud Risk Assessment and a Decision Prompt." *Behavioural Research in Accounting* 26, no. 1, pp. 131-56.

Brennan, N., and M. Mcgrath. 2007. "Financial Statement Fraud: Some Lessons from US and European Case Studies." *Australian Accounting Review* 17, no. 2, pp. 49-61.

Brinkley, D., and R. Schell. 1995. "What Is There to Worry About? An Introduction to the Computer Security Problem." *Information Security, An Integrated Collection of Essays*. Silver Spring, MD: IEEE Computer Society.

Broby, D., and P. Grieg. 2017. "The Financial Auditing of Distributed Ledgers, Blockchain and Cryptocurrencies." *Journal of Financial Transformation* 46, no. 46, p. 1755.

Brown-Liburd, H., and A.M. Vasarhelyi. 2015. "Big Data and Audit Evidence." *Journal of Emerging Technologies in Accounting* 12, no. 1, pp. 1-16.

Brown-Liburd, H., H. Issa, and D. Lombardi. 2015. "Behavioural Implications of Big Data's Impact on Audit Judgment and Decision Making and Future Research Directions." *Accounting Horizons* 29, no. 2, pp. 451-68.

Bursik, R.J. 1988. "Social Disorganization and Theories of Crime and Delinquency: Problems and Prospects." *Criminology* 26, no. 4, pp. 519-22. doi.org/10.1111/j.1745-9125.1988.tb00854.x.

Cancino, F. 2010. "The Fraud Beneath the Surface." *Internal Auditor* 67, no. 1, pp. 33-36.

Cao, M., R. Chychyla, and T. Stewart. 2015. "Big Data Analytics in Financial Statement Audits." *Accounting Horizons* 29, no. 2, pp. 423-29.

Carcello, J.V., and D.R. Hermanson. 2008. "Fraudulent Financial Reporting: How Do We Close the Knowledge Gap? Working Paper." University of Tennessee and Kennesaw State University. https://www.semanticscholar. org/paper/Fraudulent-Financial-Reporting%3A-How-Do-We-Close-the-Carcello-Hermanson/f4bfb3c2730f6cceab7d3d957aed3776da96738f#cit ing-papers, (accessed March 1, 2019).

Carcello, J.V., S.M. Beasley, D.R. Hermanson, and T.L. Neal. 2010. *Fraudulent Financial Reporting: 1998-2007.* Jersey City, NJ: Committee of Sponsoring Organizations of the Treadway Commission. https://www.coso.org/Documents/ COSO-Fraud-Study-2010-001.pdf, (accessed March 1, 2019).

Carpenter, T.D. 2008. "Audit Team Brainstorming, Fraud Risk Identification, and Fraud Risk Assessment: Implications of SAS No.99." *The Accounting Review* 82, no. 5, pp. 1119–40.

CCN. 2018. "Big Four Giant PwC Announces Blockchain Auditing Service." https:// www.ccn.com/pwc-to-provide-audit-service-for-blockchain-to-stimulate-adoption/, (accessed May 20, 2018).

Centre for Audit Quality. December 2010. "Deterring and Detecting Financial Reporting Fraud: A Platform for Actio," pp. 1-32. www.aicpa.com, (accessed January 1, 2019).

Cheffins, B. 2009. "Did Corporate Governance Fail During the 2008 Stock Market Meltdown? The Case of the S&P 500." *Business Lawyer* 65, no. 1, pp. 1-65.

Chemuturi, V.R. Winter 2008. "Are You Prepared to Assess Fraud Risk Factors?" *Pennsylvania CPA Journal* 78, no. 4, p. 1.

Chen, J., D. Cumming, W. Hou, and E. Lee. 2013. "Executive Integrity, Audit Opinion, and Fraud in Chinese Listed Firms." *Emerging Markets Review* 15, pp. 72-91.

Chen, K.Y., and R.J. Elder. 2007. "Fraud Risk Factors and the Likelihood of Fraudulent Financial Reporting: Evidence from Statement on Auditing Standards no. 43 in Taiwan," p. 28. www.ssrn.com, (accessed March 1, 2019).

Chesney, M., and Gibson-Asner, R. 2005. "Stock Options and Managers' Incentives to Cheat." www.ssrn.com, (accessed January 1, 2019).

Chhaochharia, V., and Y. Grinstein. 2007. "Corporate Governance and Firm Value: The Impact of the 2002 Governance Rules." *The Journal of Finance* 62, no. 4, pp. 1789-1825.

Choo, F., and K. Tan. 2007. "An 'American dream' Theory of Corporate Executive Fraud." *Accounting Forum* 31, pp. 203-15.

Chowdhury, S.D., and E.Z. Wang. 2009. "Institutional Activism Types and CEO Compensation: A Time-Series Analysis of Large Canadian Corporation." *Journal of Management* 35, pp. 5-36.

Chun, J.S., Y. Shin, N.J. Choi, and M.S. Kim. 2013. "How Does Corporate Ethics Contribute to Firm Financial Performance? The Mediating Role of Collective Organizational Commitment and Organizational Citizenship Behaviour." *Journal of Management* 39, no. 4, 853-77.

Cielswicz, J.K. 2012. "The Fraud Model in International Contexts: A Call to Include Societal-Level Influences in the Model." *Journal of Forensic and Investigative Accounting* 4, no. 2, pp. 214-54.

Coenen, T. 2008. *Essentials of Corporate Fraud.* Hoboken, NJ: Wiley.

Coenen, T.L. 2009. *Expert Fraud Investigation: A Step – By – Step Guide.* Hoboken, NJ: John Wiley and Sons.

Cohen, J., Y. Ding, C. Lesage, and H. Stolowy. 2010. "Corporate Fraud and Managers' Behaviour: Evidence from the Press." *Journal of Business Ethics* 95, pp. 271-315.

Coleman, J.W. 2002. *The Criminal Elite.* New York: St. Martin's Press.

Cooper, K., and I. Fargher. 2011. Accounting for Corruption: Abuse of Rank and Privilege. *Critical Perspectives on Accounting Conference*, pp. 1-34. https://ro.uow.edu.au/cgi/viewcontent.cgi?article=3208&context=commpapers.

Cornish, D.B., and R.V. Clarke. 2014. *The Reasoning Criminal: Rational Choice Perspectives on Offending.* New Brunswick, NJ and London, UK: Transaction Publishers.

Courtois, C., and Gendron, Y. 2017. "The 'Normalization' of Deviance: A Case Study on the Process Underlying the Adoption of Deviant Behaviour." *Auditing: A Journal of Practice & Theory* 36, no. 3, pp. 15-43.

Cressey, D. 1973. *Other People's Money.* Montclair, NJ: Patterson Smith.

Cressey, D.R. 1950. "The Criminal Violation of Trust." *American Sociological Review* 15, no. 6, pp. 738-40.

Cressey, D.R. 1953. *Other People's Money: A Study in the Social Psychology of Embezzlement.* Glencoe: The Free Press.

Cressey, D.R. 1960. "Limitations on Organization of Treatments in the Modern Prison. In *Theoretical studies in Social Organization of the Prison*, ed. S.L. Messinger, G.H. Grosser, G.M. Sykes, D.R. Cressey, L. Ohlin, R. McCleery and R. Cloward. New York, NY: Social Science Research Council, pp. 78-110.

Crowe, H. 2011. *Why the Fraud Triangle is No Longer Enough.* Chicago, IL: Horwath, Crowe LLP.

Cullinan, P.C., H. Du, and G.B. Wright 2008. "Is There An Association between Director Option Compensation and the Likelihood of Misstatement?" *Advances in Accounting, Incorporating Advances in International Accounting* 24, 16-23.

Cunningham, L.A. 2004. "The Appeal and Limits of Internal Controls to Fight Fraud, Terrorism, Other Ills." *Journal of Corporation Law* 29, pp. 267-336.

Dai, J., and M.A. Vasarhelyi. 2016. "Imagineering Audit 4.0." *Journal of Emerging Technologies in Accounting* 13, no. 1, pp. 1-15.

Davis, J.H., D.F. Schoorman, and L. Donaldson. 1997. "Toward a Stewardship Theory of Management." *Academy of Management Review* 22, no. 1, pp. 20-47.

Dechow, P.M., R.G. Sloan, and A.P. Sweeney. 1996. "Causes and Consequences of Earnings Manipulation: An Analysis of Firm's Subject to Enforcement Actions by the SEC." *Contemporary Accounting Research* 13, no. 1, pp. 1-36.

Dechow, P.M., W. Ge, C.R. Larson, and R.G. Sloan. 2010. Predicting material accounting misstatements. Contemporary Accounting Research, forthcoming. *AAA 2008*. Financial Accounting and Reporting Section FARS Paper. www.ssrn.com, (accessed July 31, 2018).

DeCovny, S. 2012. "The Financial Psychopath Next Door." *CFA Institute Magazine* 23, no. 2, pp. 34-35.

Dellaportas, S. 2013. "Conversations with Inmate Accountants: Motivation, Opportunity and the Fraud Triangle." *Accounting Forum* 37, no. 1, pp. 29-39.

Deloitte. 2016a. "Blockchain Technology A Game Changer in Accounting?" https://www2.deloitte.com/content/dam/Deloitte/de/Documents/Innovation/Blockchain_A%20game-changer%20in%20accounting.pdf, (accessed March 21, 2018).

Deloitte. 2016b. "Blockchain- Enigma. Paradox. Opportunity." https://www2.deloitte.com/content/dam/Deloitte/uk/Documents/Innovation/deloitte-uk-blockchain-full-report.pdf, (accessed March 21, 2018).

Deloitte. 2016c. "Bitcoin, Blockchain & Distributed Ledgers: Caught between Promise and Reality." https://www2.deloitte.com/content/dam/Deloitte/au/Images/infographics/au-deloitte-technology-bitcoin-blockchain-distributed-ledgers-180416.pdf, (accessed March 21, 2018).

Deloitte. 2016d. "Tech Trends 2016: Innovating in the Digital Era: Blockchain: Democratised Trust Distributed Ledgers and the Future of Value." https://www2.deloitte.com/content/dam/Deloitte/global/Documents/Technology/gx-tech-trends-2016-innovating-digital-era.pdf, (accessed March 21, 2018).

Dennis, H. 2017. "Forensic Accounting, Fraud Theory and, the End of the Fraud Triangle." *Journal of Theoretical Accounting Research* 12, no. 2, pp. 28-49.

Desai, N., G. Trompeter, and A. Wright. 2010. "How Does Rationalization and its Interactions with Pressure and Opportunity Affect the Likelihood of Earnings Management?" Working Paper. www.ssrn.com, (accessed July 31, 2018).

Deutschman, A. 2005. "Is Your Boss a Psychopath?" http://www.fastcompany.copm/53247/your-boss-psychopath, https://www.fastcompany.com/53247/your-boss-psychopath, (accessed December 24, 2017).

Dewing, I.P., and P.O. Russell. 2002. "UK Fund Managers, Audit Regulation and the New Accountancy Foundation: Towards a Narrowing of the Audit Expectations Gap?" *Managerial Auditing Journal* 17, no. 9, pp. 537-45.

Digital Asset. 2016. *The Digital Asset Platform: Non-Technical White Paper.* New York, NY: Digital Asset Asset Holdings, LLC.

Donald Warren, J. Jr., K.C. Moffitt, and P. Byrnes. 2015. "How Big Data Will Change Accounting." *Accounting Horizons* 29, no. 2, pp. 397-407.

Donegan, J.J., and M.W. Ganon. 2008. "Strain, Differential Association, and Coercion: Insights from the Criminology Literature on Causes of Accountant's Misconduct." *Accounting and the Public Interest* 8, no. 1, pp. 1-20.

Dorminey, J., S. Fleming, M. Kranacher, and R. Riley, 2011. "The Evolution of Fraud Theory." *American Accounting Association Annual Meeting.* Denver, pp. 1-58.

Dorminey, J., A. Fleming, M. Kranacher, and R. Riley. 2012. "The Evolution of Fraud Theory." *Issues in Accounting Education* 27, no. 2, pp. 555-79.

Dorminey, J.W., S.A. Fleming, M.J. Kranacher, and R.A. Rilley. July2010. "Beyond the Fraud Triangle: Enhancing Deterrence of Economic Crimes." *The CPA Journal* 80, no. 7, pp. 17-23.

Duarte, J., K. Kong, S. Siegel, and L. Young. 2014. "The Impact of the Sarbanes–Oxley Act on Shareholders and Managers of Foreign Firms." *Review of Finance* 18, no. 1, pp. 417-55.

Dunn, P. 1999. *Fraudulent Financial Reporting: A Deception Based on Predisposition, Motive, and Opportunity.* PhD Thesis. Boston University, Graduate School of Management.

Dunn, P. 2004. "The Impact of Insider Power on Fraudulent Financial Reporting." *Journal of Management* 30, no. 3, pp. 397-412.

Dzuranin, A C., and I. Mălăescu. 2016. "The Current State and Future Direction of IT Audit: Challenges and Opportunities." *Journal of Information Systems* 30, no. 1, pp. 7-20.

Elayan, F., J. Li, and T. Meyer. 2008. "Accounting Irregularities, Management Compensation Structure, and Information Asymmetry." *Accounting and Finance* 48, pp. 741-60.

Elder, R.J., S.M. Beasley, and A.A. Arens. 2010. *Fraud Auditing. Auditing and Assurance Services: An Integrated Approach.* 13th ed. Upper Saddle River, NJ: Pearson.

Epstein, B.J., and S. Ramamoorti. March 2016. "Auditing with 'Dark Triad' Individuals in the Executive Ranks." *The CPA Journal* 86, no. 3, pp. 14-21.

Erickson, M., M. Hanlon, and E. Maydew. 2006. "Is There a Link Between Executive Equity Incentives and Accounting Fraud?" *Journal of Accounting Research* 44, no. 1, pp. 113-43.

Favere-Marchesi, M. 2009. Cognitive Effects of Decomposition on Fraud-Risk Assessments. *CAAA Annual Conference 2009 Paper*, pp. 1-23. www.ssrn.com, (accessed April 1, 2019).

Financial Reporting Council (FRC). 2019. Developments in Audit 2019. https://www.frc.org.uk/.

Financial Services Authority. 2009. "The Turner Review a Regulatory Response to the Global Banking Crisis." March. https://www.nottingham.ac.uk/

business/businesscentres/gcbfi/documents/researchreports/paper61.pdf, (accessed April 20, 2018).

Financial Stability Board. 2017. "Financial Stability Implications from FinTech." http://www.fsb.org/wp-content/uploads/R270617.pdf, (accessed April 20, 2018).

Firth, M., O.M. Rui, and W. Wu. 2011. "Cooking the Books: Recipes and Costs of Falsified Financial Statements in China." *Journal of Corporate Finance* 17, pp. 371-90.

Fraud Act. 2006. *Chapter 35: Fraud.* London, UK: The Stationery Office Limited.

Free, C. 2015. "Looking Through the Fraud Triangle: A Review and Call for New Directions." *Meditari Accountancy Research* 23, no. 2, pp. 175-96.

Frost, K. 2012. "Top 10 Reasons Why Frauds Occur," *Metro.* Archived from the original on May 6, 2017 (accessed November 30, 2018).

Frunza, M.C. 2016. *Solving Modern Crime in Financial Markets.* 1st ed. Oxford, UK: Elsevier.

Furnham, A., S.C. Richards, and D.L. Paulhus, 2013. "The Dark Triad of Personality: A 10-Year Review." *Social and Personality Psychology Compass* 7, no. 3, pp. 199-216.

Giroux, G. 2013. *Business Scandals, Corruption & Reform. An Encyclopedia.* Vol. 1. Westport, CT: Greenwood.

Goel, S., and J. Gangolly. 2012. "Beyond the Numbers: Mining the Annual Reports for Hidden Cues Indicative of Financial Statement Fraud." *Intelligent Systems in Accounting, Finance, and Management* 19, pp. 75-89.

Golia, N. 2013. "What Big Data Means for Infrastructure Costs?" *Insurance and Technology* May, 30-31.

Gordon, E.A., E. Henry, T.T. Louwers, and B.J. Reed. March 2007. "Auditing Related Party Transactions: A Literature Overview and Research Synthesis." *Accounting Horizons* 21, no. 1.

Gottfredson, M.R., and T. Hirschi, 1990. *A General Theory of Crime.* Stanford, CA: Stanford University Press.

Gray, R., D. Owen, and C. Adams. 1996. *Accounting and Accountability; Changes and Challenges in Corporate Social and Environmental Reporting.* Harlow, UK: Prentice Hall Europe.

Greenfield, H. 2010. "The Decline of the Best: An Insider's Lessons from Lehman Brothers." *Leader to Leader* 55, pp. 30-36.

Gupta, V. 2017. "The Promise of Blockchain Is a World Without Middlemen." *Harvard Business Review Digital Articles.* https://www.hbsp.harvard.edu/product/H03HV9-PDF-ENG?Ntt=&itemFindingMethod=Recommendation&recommendedBy=H02F0M-PDF-ENG.

Ham, C., M.H. Lang, N. Seybert, and S. Wang. 2015. "CFO Narcissism and Financial Reporting Quality." https://papers.ssrn.com/sol3/papers.cfm?abstract_id=2581157, (accessed December 25, 2017).

Hasnan, S., R.A. Rahman, S. Mahenthiran. 2008. *Management Predisposition, Motive, Opportunity, and Earnings Management for Fraudulent Financial Reporting in Malaysia*, pp. 1-47. www.ssrn.com, (accessed May 1, 2019).

Hasnan, S., R. Abdul Rahman, and S. Mahenthiran. 2013. "Management Motive, Weak Governance, Earnings Management, and Fraudulent Financial Reporting: Malaysian Evidence." *Journal of International Accounting Research* 12, no. 1, pp. 1-27.

Haynie, D.L., and D.W. Osgood. 2005. "Reconsidering Peers and Delinquency: How Do Peers' Matter?" *Social Forces* 84, no. 1109, pp. 1109-30.

Henry, S., and M. Lanier. 2006. *The Essential Criminology Reader*. Boulder, CO: Westview Press.

Hochberg, Y.V., P. Sapienza, and A. Vissing-Jorgensen. 2009. "A Lobbying Approach to Evaluating the Sarbanes-Oxley Act of 2002." *Journal of Accounting Research* 47, no. 2, pp. 519-83.

Hodge, M., and L. Reid. 1971. "The Influence of Similarity between Relevant and Irrelevant Information Upon a Complex Identification Task." *Perception and Psychophysics* 10, no. 4, pp. 193-96.

Hollinger, R.C., and J.P. Clark. 1984. *Theft by Employees*. Lexington, UK: Lexington Books.

Holtfreter, K. 2005. "Fraud in US Organisations: An Examination of Control Mechanisms." *Journal of Financial Crime* 12, no. 1, pp. 88-95.

Hopwood, W.S., J.J. Leiner, and G. Young. 2008. *Forensic Accounting*. New York, NY: McGraw-Hill Irwin.

Hribar, P., T. Kravet, and R. Wilson. 2014. "A New Measure of Accounting Quality." *Review of Accounting Studies* 19, no. 1, pp. 506-38.

Huber, D.W. 2017. "Forensic Accounting, Fraud Theory, and the End of the Fraud Triangle." *Journal of Theoretical Accounting Research* 12, no. 2, pp. 28-48.

Hyperledger. 2016. "Hyperledger Whitepaper." https://blockchainlab.com/pdf/Hyperledger%20Whitepaper.pdf, (accessed April 20, 2018).

IAASB. 2016. "Exploring the Growing Use of Technology in the Audit, with a Focus on Data Analytics." *IAASB Data Analytics Working Group*. https://www.iaasb.org/publications/exploring-growing-use-technology-audit-focus-data-analytics, (accessed 20 April 2018).

IBM. 2012. "The Four V's of Big Data." https://www.ibmbigdatahub.com/infographic/four-vs-big-data#:~:text=IBM%20data%20scientists%20break%20big,and%20gives%20examples%20of%20each, (accessed April 20, 2018).

Inagaki, K. 2015a. "Japan Inc Left Shaken by Toshiba Scandal." *The Financial Times*, July 22.

Inagaki, K. 2015b. "EY's Japan Chief Quits After Toshiba Audit Fine." *The Financial Times*, December 23.

Inbar, D. February 2013. "Making the Most Out of Your Data: Big Data Opportunities." *Silicon India*, p. 35.

International Federation of Accountants. 2019. "International Code of Ethics for Professional Accountants (Including International Independence Standards." https://www.ethicsboard.org/publications/final-pronouncement-restructured-code-19, (accessed April 1, 2019).

Issa, H., and A. Kogan. 2013. A Predictive Ordered Logistic Regression Model for Quality Review of Control Risk Assessments. Working Paper. Rutgers Accounting Research Center.

Jackson, C.W. 2015. *Detecting Accounting Fraud. Analysis and Ethics*. Global ed. Ashford, UK: Pearson.

Jain, P.K., C.J. Kim, and Z. Rezaee. 2008. "The Sarbanes-Oxley Act of 2002 and Market Liquidity." *Financial Review* 43, no. 3, pp. 361-82.

Jayalakshmy, R., A. Seetharaman, and T.W. Khong. 2005. "The Changing Role of the Auditors." *Managerial Auditing Journal* 20, no. 3, pp. 249-71.

Jensen, M.C., and M.H. Meckling. 1976. "Theory of the Firm: Managerial Behavior, Agency Costs and Ownership Structure." *Journal of Financial Economics* 3, no. 4, pp. 305-60.

Johnson, E.N., J.R. Kuhn, B.A. Apostolou, and J.M. Hassell. 2013. "Auditor Perceptions of Client Narcissism as a Fraud Attitude Risk Factor." *Auditing: A Journal of Practice & Theory* 32, no. 1, pp. 203-19.

Johnson, G.G., and C.L. Rudesill. 2001. "An Investigation into Fraud Prevention and Detection of Small Businesses in the United States: Responsibilities of Auditors, Managers, and Business Owners." *Accounting Forum* 25, 1, p. 56.

Johnson, S.A., H.E. Ryan, and Tian, Y.S. 2008. "Managerial Incentives and Corporate Fraud: The Sources of Incentives Matter." www.ssrn.com, (accessed January 1, 2019).

Jo-Kranacher, M., and L. Stern. 2004. "Enhancing Fraud Detection through Education." *The CPA Journal* 74, no. 11, p. 66.

Jones, M. 2011. *Creative Accounting, Fraud and International Accounting Scandals*. London, UK: Wiley.

Kalbers, L.P. 2009. "Fraudulent Financial Reporting, Corporate Governance and Ethics: 1987-2007." *Review of Accounting and Finance* 8, no. 2, pp. 187-209.

Kamel, H., and S. Elbanna. 2010. "Assessing the Perceptions of the Quality of Reported Earnings in Egypt." *Managerial Auditing Journal* 25, no. 1, pp. 32-52.

Kang, Q., Q. Liu, and R. Qi. 2010. "The Sarbanes-Oxley Act and Corporate Investment: A Structural Assessment." *Journal of Financial Economics* 96, no. 2, pp. 291-305.

Kapardis, M.K. 2002. "A Fraud Detection Model: A Must for Auditors." *Journal of Financial Regulation and Compliance* 10, no. 3, pp. 266-78.

Kapardis, M.K., C. Christodoulou, and M. Agathocleous. 2010. "Neural Networks: The Panacea in Fraud Detection?" *Managerial Auditing Journal* 25, no. 7, pp. 659-78.

Kaptein, M. 2011. "Understanding Unethical Behaviour by Unravelling Ethical Culture." *Human Relations* 64, no. 6, pp. 843-69.

Kassem, R. 2016. *Detecting Financial Reporting Fraud: The Impact and Implications of Management Motivations for External Auditors – Evidence from the Egyptian Context* [PhD Thesis]. Loughborough, UK: Loughborough University.

Kassem, R., and A. Higson. 2012. "Financial Reporting Fraud: Are Standards' Setters and Auditors Doing Enough?" *International Journal of Business and Social Science* 3, no. 19, pp. 283-90.

Kassem, R., and A.W. Higson. 2016. "External Auditors and Corporate Corruption: Implications for Audit Regulators." *Current Issues in Auditing.*

Keay, J. 1992. *The Honourable East India Company: A History of the English East India Company.* London, UK: HarperCollins.

Kohlbeck, M., and B. Mayhew. 2004. "Related Party Transactions." http//:www.ssrn.com, (accessed January 1, 2019).

Koshy, P., D. Koshy, and P. McDaniel. 2014. "An Analysis of Anonymity in Bitcoin Using P2P Network Traffic." In *Financial Cryptography and Data Security,* ed. N. Christin and R. Safavi-Naini. Vol. 8437. Lecture Notes in Computer Science. Heidelberg: Springer Berlin.

KPMG Forensic. 2014. *Fraud Risk Management: Developing a Strategy for Prevention, Detection, and Response.* Hongkong, China: KPMG.

KPMG. 2006. *Fraud Survey 2006.* Melbourne, Australia: KPMG Forensic.

KPMG. 2016a. *Fraud and Misconduct: The Changing Landscape.* USA: KPMG. Youtube: https://www.youtube.com/watch?v=TbrH_xdwCyU

KPMG. 2016b. *Consensus, Immutable Agreement for the Internet of Value.* Delaware, USA: KPMG.

KPMG. 2016c. *Leveraging Data Analytics and Continuous Auditing Processes for Improved Audit Planning, Effectiveness, and Efficiency.* Delaware, USA: KPMG.

KPMG. 2017a. *Audit 2025, The Future Is Now.* Forbes Insights (March). Delaware, USA: KPMG.

KPMG. 2017b. *KPMG Fraud Barometer 2017.* Melbourne, Australia: KPMG.

Krahel, J.P., and W.R. Titera. 2015. "Consequences of Big Data and Formalization on Accounting and Auditing Standards." *Accounting Horizons* 29, no. 2, pp. 409-22.

Kranacher, M.J., R. Riley, and J.T. Wells. 2010. *Forensic Accounting and Fraud Examination.* 1st ed. Hoboken, NJ: John Wiley & Sons.

Kranacher, M.J., R. Riley, and J.T. Wells. 2011. *Forensic Accounting and Fraud Examination.* New York, NY: John Wiley & Sons.

Lala, S., M. Gupta, and R. Sharman. 2014. "Fraud Detection through Routine Use of CAATTs." *9th Annual Symposium on Information Assurance.* (ASIA'14), pp. 50-56.

Lansiti, M., and K. Lakhani. January/February 2017. "The Truth About Blockchain." *Harvard Business Review*, pp. 3-11 .

Le Maux, J., and D. Morin. 2011. "Black and White and Red All Over: Lehman Brothers' Inevitable Bankruptcy Splashed Across Its Financial Statements." *International Journal of Business & Social Science* 2, no. 20, pp. 39-36.

Lee, K., and M.C. Ashton. 2005. "Psychopathy, Machiavellianism, and Narcissism in the Five-Factor Model and the HEXACO Model of Personality Structure." *Personality and Individual Differences* 38, pp. 1571-82.

Levenson, M.R., K.A. Kiehl, and C.M. Fitzpatrick. 1995. "Assessing Psychopathic Attributes in a Noninstitutionalized Population." *Journal of Personality and Social Psychology* 68, no. 1, pp. 151-58.

Lioudis, N.K. 2017. "The Collapse of Lehman Brothers: A Case Study." https://www.investopedia.com/articles/economics/09/lehman-brothers-collapse.asp, (accessed November 22, 2018).

Lister, L.M. December 2007. "A Practical Approach to Fraud Risk." *Internal Auditor* 64, no. 6.

Loebbecke, J.K., M.M. Eining, and J.J. Willingham. Fall 1989. "Auditor's Experience with Material Irregularities: Frequency, Nature, and Detectability." *Auditing: A Journal of Practice & Theory* 9, no. 1, pp. 1-28.

Lokanan, M.E. 2015. "Challenges to the Fraud Triangle: Questions on Its Usefulness." *Accounting Forum* 39, no. 3, pp. 201-24.

Lord, A.T. 2010. "The Prevalence of Fraud: What Should We, As Academics, Be Doing to Address the Problem?" *Accounting and Management Information Systems* 9, no. 1, pp. 4-21.

Makkawi, B., and A. Schick. 2003. "Are Auditors Sensitive Enough to Fraud?" *Managerial Auditing Journal* 18. www.emerald.com, (accessed July 1, 2019).

Mansfield, D. 2013. "Keepin' It Clean." *NZ Marketing Magazine* July, p. 72.

Marks, J. 2009. *Playing Offense in a High-Risk Environment*. New York, NY: Crowe Horwath.

Matsueda, M.L. 1988. "The Current State of Differential Association Theory." *Crime and Delinquency* 34, no. 3, p. 277.

Mayer-Schönberger, V., and Cukier, K. 2013. *Big Data: A Revolution That Will Transform How We Live, Work, and Think*. New York, NY: Eamon Dolan/Houghton Mifflin Harcourt.

Mckee, M., and R. Santore. 2008. "Hand in the Cookie Jar: An Experimental Investigation of Equity-Based Compensation and Managerial Fraud." *Southern Economic Journal* 75, no. 1, pp. 261-78.

McKinsey. 2011. "BigData, TheNextFrontierforInnovation, CompetitionandPro-ductivity." http://www.mckinsey.com/businessfunctions/digital-mckinsey/our-insights/big-data-the-next-frontier-for-innovation, (accessed April 27, 2018).

Mehta, A. 2016. *Toshiba: Accounting Fraud.* Case Study. Brighton, MA: Harvard Business Review.

Mokhiber, R. 2007. Twenty Things You Should Know About Corporate Crime. *Inc: Taming the Giant Corporation Conference,* Washington, DC.

Mokhiber, R., and R. Weissman. 2005. *On the Rampage: Corporate Power and the Destruction of Democracy.* Corporate Focus Series. Monroe, ME: Common Courage Press.

Morales, J., Y. Gendron, and H. Guénin-Paracini. 2014. "The Construction of the Risky Individual and Vigilant Organization: A Genealogy of the Fraud Triangle." *Accounting, Organizations and Society* 39, no. 3, pp. 170-94.

Mortensen, T., R. Fisher, and G. Wines. 2012. "Students as Surrogates for Practicing Accountants: Further Evidence." *Accounting Forum* 36, no. 4, pp. 251-65.

Moyes, G.D., H.F. Mohd Din, and N. Omar. 2009. "The Effectiveness of the Auditing Standards to Detect Fraudulent Financial Reporting Activities in Financial Statement Audits in Malaysia." *International Business & Economics Research Journals* 8, no. 9, doi:10.19030/iber.v8i9.3163.

Murphy, P.R., and M.T. Dacin. 2011. "Psychological Pathways to Fraud: Understanding and Preventing Fraud in Organisations." *Journal of Business Ethics* 101, pp. 601-18.

Neuman, E. 2005. "The Impact of the Enron Accounting Scandal on Impressions of Managerial Control." *Academy of Management Best Conference Paper,* pp. 1-6.

Nijenhuis, R. 2016. *Prevention of Fraud Cases* [MBA Thesis]. Enschede, The Netherlands: University of Twente.

O'Gara, J.D. 2004. *Corporate Fraud: Case studies in Detection and Prevention.* Hoboken, NJ: John Wiley and Sons.

Oguto, E.O. 2016. "Corporate Failure and the Role of Governance: The Parmalat Scandal." *International Journal of Management and Information Technology* 11, no. 3, pp. 2747-54.

Omar, N.B., and H.F.M. Din. 2010. Fraud Diamond Risk Indicator: An Assessment of Its Importance and Usage. *2010 International Conference.* Science and Social Research (CSSR).

Owens-Jackson, L.A., D. Robinson, and S.W. Shelton. 2009. "The Association between Audit Committee Characteristics, the Contracting Process and Fraudulent Financial Reporting." *American Journal of Business* 24, no. 1, pp. 57-63.

Paulhus, D.L., and K.M. Williams. 2002. "The Dark Triad of Personality." *Journal of Research in Personality* 36, pp. 556-63.

Pavlo, W., and N. Weinberg. 2007. *Stolen Without a Gun: Confessions from Inside History's Biggest Accounting Fraud: The Collapse pf MCI WorldCom.* Tampa, FL: Ekita Books LLC.

Perols, J. 2011. "Financial Statement Fraud Detection: An Analysis of Statistical and Machine Learning Algorithms." *Auditing: A Journal of Practice & Theory* 30, no. 2, pp. 19-50.

Perols, J.L., and B.A. Lougee. 2010. "The Relation between Earnings Management and Financial Statement Fraud," *Advances in Accounting, Incorporating Advances in International Accounting.* www.elsevier.com, (accessed March 1, 2019).

Persons, O. 2012. "Stock Option and Cash Compensation of Independent Directors and Likelihood of Fraudulent Financial Reporting." *Journal of Business & Economics Studies* 18, no. 1, pp. 54-74.

Peterson, B.K., and P.E. Zikmund. May 2004. "10 Truths You Need to Know about Fraud." *Strategic Finance*, pp. 29-35.

Piquero, N.L., S.G. Tibbetts, and M.B. Blankenship. 2005. "Examining the Role of Differential Association and Techniques of Neutralization in Explaining Corporate Crime." *Deviant Behavior* 26, no. 2, pp. 159-88.

Power, M. 2013. "The Apparatus of Fraud Risk." *Accounting, Organizations and Society* 38, no. 6, pp. 525-43.

Public Company Accounting Oversight Board (PCAOB). 2005. *Consideration of Fraud in a Financial Statement Audit.* AU Section 31.

PwC. 2017. "Distributed Ledger Technology—The Genesis of a New Business Model for the Asset Management Industry." https://www.pwc.lu/en/fintech/docs/pwcfintech-distributed-ledger-technology.pdf, (accessed April 27, 2018).

Rae, D. 2016. "Beyond Bitcoin: Blockchain and the Distributed Ledger." http://www.accaglobal.com/uk/en/member/accountingbusiness/2016/04/practice/beyond-bitcoin.html, (accessed April 27, 2018).

Rae, K., and N. Subramaniam. 2008. "Quality of Internal Control Procedures: Antecedents and Moderating Effect on Organizational Justice and Employee Fraud." *Managerial Auditing Journal* 23, no. 2, pp. 104-24.

Rahman, K.M., and B. Marc. 2016. "Effective Corporate Governance and Financial Reporting in Japan." *Asian Academy of Management Journal of Accounting and Finance* 12, no. 1, pp. 89-118.

Ramamoorti, S. 2008. "The Psychology and Sociology of Fraud: Integrating the Behavioural Sciences Component into Fraud and Forensic Accounting Curricula." *Issues in Accounting Education* 23, no. 4, pp. 521-33.

Ramamoorti, S., D. Morrison, and J.W. Koletar. December 2009. "Bringing Freud to Fraud: Understanding the State of Mind of the C-level Suite/White

Collar Offender through A-B-C Analysis." *The Institute for Fraud Prevention (IFP)*, pp. 1-35.

Ramus, F., S. Rosen, C.S. Dakin, B.L. Day, M.J. Castellote, S. White, and U. Frith. 2003. "Theories of Developmental Dyslexia: Insights from a Multiple Case Study of Dyslexic Adults." *Brain* 126, no. 4, pp. 841-65.

Rezaee, Z. 2003. *Financial Statement Fraud: Prevention and Detection.* New York, NY: Wiley.

Rezaee, Z. 2005. "Causes, Consequences, and Deterrence of Financial Statement Fraud." *Critical Perspectives on Accounting* 16, pp. 227-98.

Rezaee, Z., and R. Riley. 2010. *Financial Statement Fraud: Prevention and Detection.* 2nd ed. Hoboken, NJ: John Wiley & Sons, Inc.

Riemer, K., E. Hafermalz, A. Roosen, N. Boussand, H. El Aoufi, D. Mo, and A. Kosheliev. 2017. "The Fintech Advantage: Harnessing Digital Technology, Keeping the Customer in Focus," *The Sydney eScholarship Repository.* https://ses.library.usyd.edu.au/handle/2123/16259, (accessed April 27, 2018).

Robins, N. 2007. "This Imperious Company: The English East India Company and Its Legacy for Corporate Accountability." *Journal of Corporate Citizenship* no. 25, pp. 31-42.

Ronson, J. 2011. *The Psychopath Test: A Journey through the Madness Industry.* New York, NY: Penguin Group.

Rosner, R.L. 2003. "Earnings Manipulation in Failing Firms." *Contemporary Accounting Research* 20, no. 2, p. 367.

Ryan, H., and R. Wiggins. 2004. "Who is in Whose Pocket? Director Compensation, Board Independence, and Barriers to Effective Monitoring." *Journal of Financial Economics* 73, no. 3, pp. 497-525.

Scapens, R.W. 2004. *Doing Case Study Research. The Real-Life Guide to Accounting Research.* Oxford, UK: Elsevier.

Schimmenti, A., P.J. Jonason, A. Passanisi, L. La Marca, N. Di Dio, and A.M. Gervasi. 2017. "Exploring the Dark Side of Personality: Emotional Awareness, Empathy, and the Dark Triad Traits in an Italian Sample." *Current Psychology* 38, pp. 100-109.

Schnatterly, K. 2010. "Increasing Firm Value Through Detection and Prevention of White-collar Crime." In *Handbook of Top Management Teams*, F. Bournois, J. Duval-Hamel, S. Roussillon, and J.L. Scaringella (eds). London, UK: Palgrave Macmillan, pp. 674–81.

Schouten, R. March 14, 2012. "Psychopaths on Wall Street," *Harvard Business Review.* https://hbr.org/2012/03/psychopaths-on-wall-street.

Schrand, C.M., and S.L. Zechman. 2012. "Executive Overconfidence and the Slippery Slope to Financial Misreporting." *Journal of Accounting and Economics* 53, no. 1, pp. 311-29.

SEC. 2003. "Report of Investigation by The Special Investigative Committee of the Board of Directors of Worldcom, Inc." https://www.sec.gov/Archives/edgar/data/723527/000093176303001862/dex991.htm, (accessed November 16, 2018).

Segato, L. 2006. "A Comparative Analysis of Shareholder protections in Italy and the United States: Parmalat as a Case Study." *Northwestern Journal of International Law & Business* 26, no. 2, pp. 373-446.

Sen, P. 2007. "Ownership Incentives and Management Fraud." *Journal of Business Finance & Accounting* 34, no. 7, pp. 1123-40.

Shanmugam, J.K., M.H.C. Haat, and A. Ali. 2012. "An Exploratory Study of Internal Control and Fraud Prevention Measures in SMEs." *Small* 100, no. 18, pp. 90-99.

Sheikh, F.M. 2017. *The Corporate Governance Cosmos.* Presentation. 3rd Annual MBA Symposium. Salford, UK: Salford Business School.

Sheikh, F.M. 2020. *IFAC Ethical Triangle.* Salford, UK: Salford Business School.

Shilit, H.M., and J. Perler. 2018 *Financial Shenanigans.* New York, NY: McGraw Hill.

Simpson, S.S. 2002. *Corporate Crime, Law, and Social Control.* Cambridge Studies in Criminology. Cambridge: Cambridge University Press.

Skousen, C.J., and C.J. Wright. 2006. "Contemporaneous Risk Factors and the Prediction of Financial Statement Fraud." www.ssrn.com, (accessed July 31, 2018).

Skousen, C.J., and Twedt, B.J. 2010. "Fraud Score Analysis in Emerging Markets." *Cross Cultural Management* 16, no. 3, pp. 301-16.

Skousen, C.J., K.R. Smith, and C.J. Wright. 2009. "Detecting and Predicting Financial Statement Fraud: The Effectiveness of the Fraud Triangle and SAS No. 99." *Advances in Financial Economics* 13, no. 1, pp. 53-81.

Smith, J.L. May 2010. "HealthSouth Co-Founder Knows How Greed Grows on You." *Las Vegas Review-Journal.*

Soltani, B. 2007. *Corporate Fraud, Corporate Scandals, and External Auditing. Auditing: An International Approach.* Edinburgh: Pearson Education Limited.

Sorensen, J.E., and T.L. Sorensen. 1980. "Detecting Management Fraud: Some Organisational Strategy for the Independent Auditor." In *Management Fraud: Detection and Deterrence*, ed. R.K. Elliott and J.J. Willingham. Princeton, NJ: Petrocelli Books.

South Coast Today. 2015. "Editorial Roundup: The Yomiuri Shimbun – Improper Accounting, Tardy Disclosure Sparked Toshiba Share Price Plunge." http://www.southcoasttoday.com/article/20150526/OPINION/, (accessed November 22, 2018).

Sterling, T.F. 2002. *The Enron Scandal.* New York, NY: Nova Science Publishers, Inc.

Stevens, G.W., J.K. Deuling, and A.A. Armenakis. 2012. "Successful Psychopaths: Are They Unethical Decision-Makers and Why?" *Journal of Business Ethics* 105, pp. 139-49.

Sutherland, E.H. 1937. *The Professional Thief*. Chicago, IL: The university of Chicago Press.

Sutherland, E.H., and W.C. Crime. 1949. *White Collar Crimes*. 1st ed. New York, NY: Holt.

Sutherland, E.H., and D.R. Cressey. 1960. *Principles of Criminology*. 6th ed. Chicago, IL: Lippincott.

Swartz, M. 2003. *Power Failure: The Inside Story of the Collapse of Enron*. New York, NY: Doubleday.

Tapscott, D., and A. Tapscott. 2016. "The Impact of the Blockchain Goes Beyond Financial Services." *Harvard Business Review Digital Articles*. https://hbr.org/2016/05/the-impact-of-the-blockchain-goes-beyond-financial-services.

The Financial Reporting Council. 2016. "The UK Code of Corporate Governance." https://www.frc.org.uk/getattachment/ca7e94c4-b9a9-49e2-a824-ad76a322873c/UK-Corporate-Governance-Code-April-2016.pdf, (accessed January 1, 2019).

The Guardian. 2017. https://www.theguardian.com/business/2017/mar/28/tesco-agrees-fine-serious-fraud-office-accounting-scandal, (accessed September 1, 2019).

The Japan News. December 8, 2015. "¥7.3 Billion Fine Sought for Toshiba Over Accounting Fraud." https://www.japantimes.co.jp/news/2015/12/25/business/corporate-business/toshiba-fined-record-%C2%A57-3-billion-over-accounting-scandal/.

Toshiba Corporation. 2015. "Investigation Report – Summary." http://www.toshiba.co.jp/about/ir/en/news/20150725_1.pdf, (accessed November 23, 2018).

Trompeter, G.M., T.D. Carpenter, N. Desai, K.L. Jones, and R.A. Riley Jr. 2013. "A Synthesis of Fraud-Related Research." *Auditing: A Journal of Practice & Theory* 32, no. 1, pp. 287-321.

Troy, C., K. Smith, and M. Domino. 2011. "CEO Demographics and Accounting Fraud: Who Is More Likely to Rationalize Illegal Acts?" *Strategic Organization* 9, no. 4, pp. 259-82.

Tugas, F.C. 2012. "Exploring a New Element of Fraud: A Study on Selected Financial accounting Fraud Cases in the World." *American International Journal of Contemporary Research* 2, no. 6, 112-12.

Uddin, N. 2000. *CFO Intentions to Report Fraudulently on Financial Statements*. PhD in Management Program, Rutgers, The State University of New Jersey.

Uddin, N., and P.R. Gillett. 2002. "The Effects of Moral Reasoning and Self-Monitoring on CFO Intentions to Report Fraudulently on Financial Statements." *Journal of Business Ethics* 40, pp. 15-32.

Van Echtelt, F.E., F. Wynstra, A.J. Van Weele, and G. Duysters. 2008. "Managing Supplier Involvement in New Product Development: A Multiple-Case Study*." *Journal of Product Innovation Management* 25, no. 2, pp. 180-20.

Van Vlasselaer, V., T. Eliassi-Rad, L. Akoglu, M. Snoeck, and B. Baesens. 2016. "Gotcha! Network-based Fraud Detection for Social Security Fraud." *Management Science* 63, no. 9, pp. 2773-3145.

Vaughn, D. 1983. *Controlling Unlawful Organizational Behaviour*. Chicago, IL: University of Chicago Press.

Verschoor, C.C. 1998. "A Study of the Link between a Corporation's Financial Performance and Its Commitment to Ethics." *Journal of Business Ethics* 17, no. 13, pp. 1509-16.

Vona, L.W. 2008. *Fraud Risk Assessment: Building a Fraud Audit Program*. Hoboken, NJ: John Wiley and Sons.

Wall Street Journal. 2012. "Psychos on Wall Street." http://on.wsj.com/1mxrhIY, (accessed December 24, 2017).

Wall, J., and T.J. Fogarty. 2016. "Foxes in the Henhouse: An Exploratory Inquiry into Financial Markets Fraud." *Journal of Forensic and Investigative Accounting* 8, no. 1, pp. 120-39.

Weld, L., P. Bergevin, and L. Magrath. 2004. "Anatomy of a Financial Fraud." *The CPA Journal* 74, no. 10, pp. 44-49.

Well, A.D. 1971. "The Influence of Irrelevant Information on Speeded Classification Tasks." *Perception and Psychophysics* 10, no. 2, pp. 79-84.

Wells, J.T. February 2004. "New Approaches for Fraud Deterrence." *Journal of Accountancy*. https://www.journalofaccountancy.com/issues/2004/feb/newapproachestofrauddeterrence.html.

Wells, J.T. 2005. "New Approaches to Fraud Deterrence." *Business Credit* 107, no. 2, pp. 33-36.

Wells, J.T. 2005. *Principles of Fraud Examination*. Hoboken, NY: John Wiley and Sons.

Wells, J.T. 2011. *Financial Statement Fraud Casebook: Baking the Ledgers and Cooking the Books*. Hoboken, NY: John Wiley & Sons.

Whittington, R., and K. Pany. 2012. *Principles of Auditing and Other Assurance Services*. 17th ed. New York, NY: McGraw-Hill Irwin.

Wilks, T.J., and M.F. Zimbelman. 2004. "Using Game Theory and Strategic Reasoning Concepts to Prevent and Detect Fraud." *Accounting Horizons* 18, no. 3, pp. 173–84.

Willot, S., S. Griffin, and M. Torrance. 2006. "Snakes and Ladders: Upper-Middle Class Male Offenders Talk about Economic Crime." *Criminology* 39, no. 2, pp. 441–66.

Wittgenstein, L. 1953. *Philosophical Investigations*. Trans. G.E.M. Anscombe. New York, NY: Macmillan.

Wolfe, D.T., and D.R. Hermanson. 2004 "The Fraud Diamond: Considering the Four Elements of Fraud." *The CPA Journal* 74, no. 12, pp. 38-42.

Woodcock, D. 2015. "Accounting Fraud: Down, But Not Out." *Law 360*. New York. www.jonesday.com/accounting-fraud-down-but-not-out-ilaw-360i-09-11-2015, (accessed December 22, 2017).

Woodward, J.D. Jr., N.M. Orlans, and P.T. Higgins. 2003. *Biometrics: Identity Assurance in the Information Age*. Santa Monica, CA: McGraw-Hill.

Zahra, S.A., R.L. Priem, and Rasheed, A.A. 2005. "The Antecedents and Consequences of Top Management Fraud." *Journal of Management* 31, no. 6, pp. 803-28.

Zhang, J., X. Yang, and D. Appelbaum. 2015. "Toward Effective Big Data Analysis in Continuous Auditing." *Accounting Horizons* 29, no. 2, pp. 469-76.

About the Author

Faisal Sheikh is an economics graduate and a qualified accountant (fellow of the Association of Chartered Certified Accountants, fellow of the Institute of Financial Accountants, and fellow of the Institute of Public Accountants (Australia)) with an excess of 20 years' professional accounting/auditing/consulting experience gained primarily in the small and medium enterprises and the (international) not-for-profit sector. He has also worked for the Big Four firms in the UK and overseas. Faisal has held lecturer/assistant professorships and academic management posts with several leading UK business schools and is currently a lecturer at Salford Business School (SBS), where he is actively researching accounting fraud. This is Faisal's second book with Business Expert Press and his first title, *A Refresher in Financial Accounting*, has been well received by students and university libraries across the world. Faisal is peer-reviewed and has published extensively in accountancy trade journals such as the *Financial Accountant*, which has a global readership of 40,000 and is also a listed author with the American Institute of Certified Public Accountants. He is a passionate teacher and has won Inspirational Teacher of the Year 2012–13 and 2013–2014 while working for Sheffield Hallam University. Business engagement remains one of his fortes and consequently he has written many press releases and op-eds for SBS. Faisal is a nationally and internationally respected accounting curriculum advisor and external examiner. He has been an external panellist representing UK universities in Bahrain, China, Egypt, Singapore, Sri Lanka, and Malaysia. He is a Bollywood enthusiast, runs regularly, and loves cooking for his wife and three little girls.

Index

OTHER TITLES IN OUR FINANCIAL ACCOUNTING, AUDITING, AND TAXATION COLLECTION

Mark Bettner, Bucknell University, Michael Coyne, Fairfield University, and Rob Sawyers, North Carolina State University (Taxation Topics), *Editors*

- *Sustainability Performance and Reporting* by Irene M. Herremans
- *Forensic Accounting and Financial Statement Fraud, Volume I, Fundamentals of Forensic Accounting* by Zabihollah Rezaee
- *Forensic Accounting and Financial Statement Fraud, Volume II, Forensic Accounting Performance* by Zabi Rezaee
- *Applications of Accounting Information Systems* by David M. Shapiro
- *A Non-Technical Guide to International Accounting* by Roger Hussey
- *The Tax Aspects of Acquiring a Business, Second Edition* by W. Eugene Seago
- *The Story Underlying the Numbers: A Simple Approach to Comprehensive Financial Statements Analysis* by S. Veena Iyer
- *Pick a Number: The U.S. and International Accounting, 2e,* by Roger Hussey
- *Using Accounting & Financial Information: Analyzing, Forecasting, and Decision Making, 2e* by Mark S. Bettner
- *Corporate Governance in the Aftermath of the Global Financial Crisis: Relevance and Reforms, Volume I* by Zabihollah Rezaee
- *Corporate Governance in the Aftermath of the Global Financial Crisis: Functions and Sustainability, Volume II* by Zabihollah Rezaee
- *Corporate Governance in the Aftermath of the Global Financial Crisis: Gatekeeper Functions, Volume III* by Zabihollah Rezaee
- *Corporate Governance in the Aftermath of the Global Financial Crisis: Emerging Issues in Corporate Governance, Volume IV* by Zabihollah Rezaee
- *Accounting Fraud: Maneuvering and Manipulation, Past and Present, 2e* by Gary Giroux
- *A Refresher in Financial Accounting* by Faisal Sheikh
- *Accounting History and the Rise of Civilization, Volume I* by Gary Giroux
- *Accounting History and the Rise of Civilization, Volume II* by Gary Giroux

Concise and Applied Business Books

The Collection listed above is one of 30 business subject collections that Business Expert Press has grown to make BEP a premiere publisher of print and digital books. Our concise and applied books are for...

- Professionals and Practitioners
- Faculty who adopt our books for courses
- Librarians who know that BEP's Digital Libraries are a unique way to offer students ebooks to download, not restricted with any digital rights management
- Executive Training Course Leaders
- Business Seminar Organizers

Business Expert Press books are for anyone who needs to dig deeper on business ideas, goals, and solutions to everyday problems. Whether one print book, one ebook, or buying a digital library of 110 ebooks, we remain the affordable and smart way to be business smart. For more information, please visit **www.businessexpertpress.com**, or contact **sales@businessexpertpress.com**.

www.ingramcontent.com/pod-product-compliance
Lightning Source LLC
Chambersburg PA
CBHW061327220326
41599CB00026B/5077